BILLY HUGHES

Published by Black Inc.
Black Inc. is an imprint of Bookman Press Pty Ltd
227 Collins Street
Melbourne Victoria 3000

First published by The Macmillan Company of Australia Pty Ltd
in 1979. Re-published in 1983

Copyright © Donald Horne 1979

Introduction © Frank Moorhouse 2000

All rights reserved.
No part of this publication may be reproduced, stored in a retrieval system, or transmitted in any form by any means electronic, mechanical, photocopying, recording or otherwise without the prior consent of the publishers.

National Library of Australia Cataloguing

Horne, Donald, 1921-
Billy Hughes

ISBN 1 86395 162 8

1. Hughes, Billy, 1862-1952 2. Prime ministers - Australia - Biography. 3. Australia - Politics and government - 1901-1945. I. Title (Series: Prime ministers series; 7)

994.04092

BILLY HUGHES

DONALD HORNE

With an Introduction by
Frank Moorhouse

Emeritus Professor Donald Horne has written over twenty books, ranging from social critique to history, autobiography and fiction. *The Little Digger: A Biography of Billy Hughes* was first published in 1979. Donald's latest book *Into the Open: Memoirs, 1958-1999* was published in April 2000 by HarperCollins.

Frank Moorhouse is the author of twelve books of fiction and one non-fiction book as well as many published essays. He has won a number of literary prizes including the Australian Literature Society's Gold Medal for *Forty-Seventeen*. *Grand Days* won the Adelaide Festival National Prize for fiction. In 1985 he was made a member of the Order of Australia for services to literature.

Contents

INTRODUCTION BY FRANK MOORHOUSE 7

PORTRAIT OF A LEGEND 15

WILL HUGHES, SOCIALIST 17

W. M. HUGHES, LABOR LEADER 54

BILLY HUGHES, PATRIOT 94

BILLY HUGHES, RAT 120

THE LITTLE DIGGER 148

OLD BILLY 167

ACKNOWLEDGEMENTS 185

INDEX 189

William Morris Hughes—
'The Little Digger'

> 'My fifty-eight years in parliament have covered the most eventful in all human history—years which have seen the two greatest wars man has ever seen, and revolutionary changes in every phase of our national, economic, political, scientific and social lives.'
>
> William Morris Hughes at his 90th birthday, 1952.

William Morris Hughes was a member of parliament (either state and federal) for fifty-eight years—and during that time was expelled from three political parties and instrumental in forming three new parties.

He was expelled from the ALP in 1916 for supporting conscription; from the National Party in 1929 for voting against it in a vote of no confidence; and expelled from the United Australia Party in 1944 for continuing to serve on the Advisory War Council after his party had walked out.

But he joined the Liberal Party (which replaced the UAP after the war) and stayed on in parliament until his death.

He became Labor prime minister in 1915, in the midst of World War One, at the age of fifty-three.

Hughes was a mixture of positions, not all of which eventually fitted with the Labor Party he had helped to establish.

He was a believer in the British Empire as a political arrangement only if the dominions had a say in the decision making at Empire level, and he was a believer in a strong military and favoured the Swiss model of a citizen army based on compulsory military training for all men.

He was a pioneer of the new Labor Party and a pioneering trade unionist, forming the Waterside Workers Federation and helping to form other unions as well.

Conscription for military service was a passionately divisive issue among Labor supporters. Although at the core, conscription was a humanist issue—that is, people should not be made to fight in wars they did not believe in nor when they were pacifists—during World War One it became entangled in other emotive issues.

Firstly, the Labor Party had been struggling to find a defence policy that did not rely on a large standing army which they historically saw as being an instrument used to oppress workers and to further imperialist ambitions. There were also more general anti-military sentiments in the Labor movement which argued that all soldiers were brothers and should lay down their arms when forced to fight each other or, as in the case of John Curtin (to be Labor prime minister in World War Two), a belief that there had to be better ways to solve international disputes than war. Curtin argued for an international general strike of German and Allied workers to stop the fighting.

Those with Irish sentiments opposed conscription because it forced them to fight in a 'British' war. Those who saw World War One as simply a British 'Imperialist War' aimed at extending British power also opposed conscription.

Those who were for it argued that it was the most fair and efficient way to raise an army—it meant that no one (except conscientious objectors) could avoid sharing the risks of war and that forward planning of the war did not depend on the unreliability, and expense, of recruiting volunteers.

Hughes saw it as a way for Australia to play a full and effective part in the war.

The conscription issue split the Labor Party. Hughes argued that it was a conflict also over the sovereignty of parliament. The Labor Party did not oppose conscription in its platform and nor had federal conference taken any resolutions against it. Hughes argued that it was a group of Labor officials dictating to the government of the day. This was to be a continuous issue in the Labor Party to the current day with the charge that Labor parliamentarians are dictated to by 'faceless men' behind the scenes.

For Hughes, it was more particularly a challenge to the supreme leadership of the office of prime minister.

The Labor Party attracted many different radical positions and had trouble finding single positions on many issues. During these early years, it struggled to find a dependable solidarity—to ensure that those members elected as Labor members stuck to Labor policy. The state and federal ALP policy conferences were an attempt to hammer out a single policy which would bind Labor politicians. The Labor Party pledge, which all elected Labor members swore, bound Labor politicians to the policies of the conferences.

The Labor Party, as does all parties, had problems with harmonising the party platform—that is, its long-term aims and party principles, those ideals seen as beyond compromise—and the pragmatic demands of day-to-day government where issues arise which have not necessarily been considered by the party.

A political party will usually sideline its platform goals and compromise to remain in power. Hughes was a fairly pragmatic politician, more interested in what would achieve a desirable result—for example, successful and swift conclusion to the war—rather than principles. In this he was, in many ways, a forerunner of the modern politician.

He was also one of the early prime ministers who contributed significantly to the idea of the dominating role of prime minister, of strong single leadership. He remarked, 'my fountain pen is the constitution'.

One of his most dramatic acts was to buy a fleet of ships

in France during his visit there, on his own initiative without reference to cabinet or parliament. These were to be used to shift Australian agricultural produce to Europe which had been held up by lack of shipping. The ships became the Commonwealth Shipping Line.

And by his role at the Peace Conference after World War One, he was the first prime minister to define an independent position and voice for Australia in world affairs. He was a very significant political player in Australian history.

***

William Hughes was born in London but after his mother died when he was seven, grew up in Wales where he went to school for ten years and did some training as an assistant teacher. His father was a carpenter.

During his youth, Hughes was also a part-time soldier in the Royal Fusiliers.

At twenty-two, he migrated to Australia and worked as an itinerant rural worker, eventually finding his way to Sydney where he married the daughter of his landlady, Elizabeth Cutts, and set up shop in Balmain (she died in 1906 and Hughes remarried to Mary Ethel Campbell five years later).

The shop sold many things, including books and political pamphlets and it eventually became a meeting place for those interested in political affairs.

Hughes started as a believer in the single-tax theories of Henry George before moving to a vague socialist position. Simply, Henry George argued that land was the basic wealth of the economy and a tax on all land should finance the workings of government. It was one of many radical social theories circulating at the turn of the century which found their way into the emerging Labor Party.

Hughes became active in the Labor Party and won a seat in the New South Wales parliament in 1894 at the age of thirty-two.

He initially opposed federation but changed his position and was elected to the first federal parliament from the seat of West Sydney. He was to remain in parliament until his death at ninety.

In line with his party, Hughes was a fierce supporter of the White Australia Policy.

In 1915, when the Labor prime minister, Andrew Fisher, resigned because of poor health, Hughes was elected as prime minister.

He was determined to prosecute the war with all the resources and manpower that Australia could muster in the spirit of Fisher's wartime slogan, 'To the last man and to the last shilling'. This caused those in the party who were suspicious of militarism to turn against him.

He visited the United Kingdom in 1916 and returned convinced of the need for conscription in Australia so that adequate reinforcements could be sent to the war. He couldn't legislate for conscription because the majority of senators were opposed to it, and instead he went to the people with a referendum. It was narrowly defeated. He was then expelled from the ALP and with other Labor members who supported him, formed a new party—the National Party or a 'win-the-war' party.

Defeated in the senate, he called an election and his new party won a sweeping victory in both the lower house and the senate. Hughes had to change his seat at this election, moving to Bendigo, in Victoria, away from his solid, Labor-voting, inner-city seat in Sydney. This was a crucial point in Hughes' life. According to one of his biographers, L. F. Fitzhardinge, 'Hughes, cut off from his political, social, and even geographical roots, expelled by the party and the union which had been such a large part of his life, distrusted by his new supporters, never...regained the authority and confidence of his early days.'

Again in 1917 he put the conscription question to referendum and lost heavily. During the campaign, Hughes was hit by a tomato thrown from the crowd and the Queensland police sergeant present refused to arrest the man. Following this incident, Hughes formed the Commonwealth Police. He resigned as prime minister but was commissioned again to form a government.

Looking back now, conscription, as important as it was as an issue 'of the day', seems to be a side-issue to the major movements in Australian history.

Because of his total support for the Australian troops fighting overseas, Hughes was made an 'honorary soldier' by some of them when he visited the front in France and given the nickname of 'The Little Digger', a name which became widely used, even after his death.

At the end of the war, he was a noisy and influential figure at the Peace Conference in Paris, being away from Australia a year in order to attend it. He successfully demanded that Australia attend the conference as an independent nation and not as part of the British Empire Group.

He was forming a suspicion of Japanese political and military ambitions and fought against them for control of Papua New Guinea (formerly controlled by Germany). He also opposed the addition of a racial equality clause to the League of Nations covenant, fearing that it would mean that all nations, including the Japanese, had a right to migrate to Australia. He feared this would undermine the White Australia Policy. At the conference, Hughes won on all the major issues which he considered important to Australia.

The election of 1922 gave the Country Party the balance of power and they refused to work with Hughes. He resigned and Stanley Bruce became prime minister. Hughes was not in the ministry.

He eventually led a revolt against Bruce and was expelled from the National Party which he had formed. Consequently, he formed yet another party, the Australian Party, and for a time supported the Labor government of James Scullin.

This new party eventually disintegrated and he joined the United Australia Party which had replaced the old

National Party and was led by Joseph Lyons (who had also been expelled from the Labor Party).

He continued to press defence issues with growing suspicion of Japan and Germany. He opposed appeasement of Hitler.

In 1939 Hughes went back into the ministry as attorney-general and then minister for Navy and was elected deputy leader of the party.

The Labor government of 1941 formed an Advisory War Council made up of representatives from all the parties in the parliament and Hughes served on it. He was again expelled, this time from the UAP, for remaining on the council after his party walked out.

After the war, he joined the new Liberal Party which replaced the UAP, taking the seat of Bradfield in Northern Sydney.

At his ninetieth birthday party, the then prime minister, Robert Menzies, said that Hughes had, during a long political lifetime, adorned every political party in the parliament.

'Not the Country Party,' Artie Fadden, leader of the Country Party, interjected.

'Had to draw the line somewhere,' the ninety-year-old Hughes riposted.

He died shortly after his ninetieth birthday.

Further reading
The major work done on Hughes is the two-volume biography, *William Morris Hughes*, by L. F. Fitzhardinge, Angus and Robertson, 1979.

Other sources:
The Diplomatic Battles of Billy Hughes, Peter Spartalis, Hale and Iremonger, 1983; *The Great Professional*, Malcolm Booker, McGraw Hill, 1980.

Hughes own books are:
The Splendid Adventure, 1929; *The Price of Peace*, 1934; *Australia and the War Today*, 1935; *Crusts and Crusades*, 1947; and *Politicians and Potentates*, 1950.

See also:
Alfred Deakin, J. A. La Nauze, Melbourne University Press, Melbourne, 1965 (two volumes); *Lion and Kangaroo*, Gavin Souter, William Collins, Sydney, 1976; *Penguin Atlas of World History*, volume two, Hermann Kinder and Werner Hilgermann, Penguin Books, London, 1978; *The Macmillan Dictionary of Australian Politics*, Dean Jaensch and Max Teichmann, Macmillan, Melbourne, 1979; *A History of Australia*, volume 5, C. M. H. Clark, Melbourne University Press, Melbourne, 1981; *The Macquarie Book of Events*, Bryce Fraser, Macquarie Library, Sydney, 1983; *The Australian Dictionary of Biography*, vol. 9, ed.s Bede Nairn and Geoffrey Serle, Melbourne University Press, Melbourne, 1983; *The Oxford History of Australia*, volume 4, Stuart Macintyre, Oxford University Press, Melbourne, 1986; *Acts of Parliament*, Gavin Souter, Melbourne University Press, Melbourne, 1988; *Australia's Commonwealth Parliament*, G. S. Reid and Martyn Forest, Melbourne University Press, Melbourne, 1989; *What Happened When*, Anthony Barker, Allen & Unwin, Sydney, 1996; *The Year Book of Australia*, various years, Australian Bureau of Statistics, Canberra.

Frank Moorhouse

Introduction

Portrait of a Legend

❧   This book is not a biography, but a 'portrait', an attempt to cast up images of a person in narration, anecdotes, highlights, close-ups. However it is not *Billy Hughes—the Man Behind the Politician* nor *The Love Life of Billy Hughes*. (These would be two extremely short books.) It is a political portrait. Insofar as it is concerned with Hughes's personality, the book is concerned with the grandeurs and miseries of the brutish life of a politician. With Hughes there is also a special concern that makes him remarkable among all Australian politicians: *how did a man like this become a living legend, seen by many Australians as epitomising the values of a whole nation?*

It is also a social portrait, of W. M. Hughes and the hard times that made possible the creation of 'Billy Hughes', his alter ego. It takes up some of the great themes of the twentieth century, put into an Australian context—in particular, the growth of the labour movement, the explosion of imperialism, and the shameful disasters of war. Through the extraordinary story of Hughes's life Australians can contemplate some of the roads by which Australia became what it is.

Hughes was an illusionist; he was an orator and writer who summoned up magical shapes (in this sense he was an artist) and an epic enough liar to play some part in the making of his own legend, even if the legend was largely made for him by the horror of the times he passed through. For this reason the words he used are an essential part of his story. That is why in this book there are quite large lumps from his speeches and writings: readers can see the kinds of shapes Hughes cast up. One could no more provide a portrait of Hughes without quoting from his rhetoric than one could provide a portrait of Henry Lawson without quoting from his verse and short stories. Although the visions may have been different, both of them helped create views of Australia.

There are problems in projecting rhetoric: usually if you paraphrase a word-conjuror's argument much of the colour drains out of the keywords and phrases (yet in a sense these are the main argument) but on the other hand if you quote extracts verbatim you cannot summarise the whole argument. What I have done is to paraphrase, but by bringing together typical phrases, sentences and paragraphs from Hughes. By this means I hope I have been able to project in a few paragraphs both the rational argument and the emotional flavour of a whole set of speeches and articles, even a whole book. The passages where this device has been used have been italicised. Most of these passages are related to Hughes, but on a few occasions (where indicated) the device has also been used for the rhetoric of other people.

I read a great number of contemporary accounts and a great amount of contemporary controversy; I also read, or re-read, a number of secondary sources. A few passages in the book come from private information. The section I have hesitated over most is the account on page 105 of Hughes replacing Fisher: this is based on a perhaps faulty memory of some hearsay, and on some conjecture.

I should like to thank Carmel Lilley, Carol Dressler and Pamela Watson for typing and Conal Condren, J. R. McClelland, Barbara Mobbs and Patricia Rolfe for reading the manuscript and giving reactions.

In particular I should like to thank Geoff Dutton for giving me the idea of writing a book about Hughes and my wife Myfanwy Horne for her invaluable and indefatigable criticisms.

Chapter 1

Will Hughes, Socialist

❧ Among the buildings labelled Bistro and Car Wash and Antiques and Continental Tailor, many of the old boarding house terraces are still there in Sydney's Flinders Street. A few have even kept up with the times—one now calls itself a motel; another is painted mulberry brown as if it were an advertising agency; another, like an espresso bar of the 1950s, displays a rubber plant. But most haven't kept up: cast iron has been pulled off verandahs and replaced with fibro; paint has been left to flake gently away; and in front gardens there are still the exotics familiar to Sydney in the late nineteenth century—palms, a locquat tree, frangipani. In the mid 1880s when he was living in this street of boarding houses, Will Hughes, a skinny little immigrant from London, a man of many jobs, took to wife his landlady's daughter.

Beyond Flinders Street a wide six-lane boulevard now sweeps between ceremonial rows of poplars and Moreton Bay figs—Anzac Parade, commemorating the war thirty years later of which Hughes, having become prime minister of Australia, was to be the loudest advocate, and for which Australia raised an army of nearly a tenth of its total population. Of that army, almost one in two was to be wounded and one in five killed.

In his role as 'Billy Hughes', or 'the Little Digger', Will Hughes was to become something rare for politicians in Australia: a living legend. It was not from the stereotype of the tall, lean sun-bronzed bushman or lifesaver, but from this deaf, dyspeptic British immigrant, his little body all parchment skin and brittle bone, that many Australians were to confirm their ideas of what Australia should be. Even though he has been dead since 1952, the memory of him returns to Sydney annually, on Anzac Day, in the form of a hat—a digger's hat, a sprig of rosemary in its puggaree, placed on the chair from which, when he was old, he would watch the procession. He was to become a legend in another way. Because he presided over the Labor Party's first great splintering, in 1916, he became for some as necessary a villain as for others he was a hero. Hughes is such a central figure in Labor Party demonology that in 1971 a Labor leader could still say that Hughes alone debauched Australian politics for the whole between-the-wars generation, totally demoralising, in turn, both political parties.

The man himself is a good story, full of the twists of politics—with his sardonic ironies and sharpness he could be written into *The Threepenny Opera*—but what really matters is that through him we can see into the mysteries of two developments of enormous importance in Australia in the twentieth century: as hero, Hughes leads us to the world of the Returned Men, the Diggers' world that settled so much of what Australia was to become; and, as demon, Hughes shows us the world of the Australian labour movement, and its potential convulsions. He helped 'create' a certain kind of Australia; but he also became a symbol of the hatreds that could lie under its apparent complacency.

Because of his almost unparalleled talents as an illusionist, he provides a problem in how to begin a story about him. With his itch for an audience and his gargantuan appetite for lying, he turned his early days into mythic sagas of hardship or short killertales of amusing trickeries—in a sense he was mad, living out his own unrealities—so that often one cannot see the little man himself through the legendary play of his shadows.

There is a mid-eighties photograph to look at...a sharp little face with big ears, a large, clean-shaven upper lip poised confidently over a slightly open mouth. Bright eyes stare out arrogantly...L. F. Fitzhardinge, his official biographer, could not find even the marriage certificate to turn over, as at least one document from his early life to show that something Hughes claimed to have happened did actually happen. We know very little about Elizabeth Cutts, the landlady's daughter, although we do know that their relationship was to end so sadly that even Hughes the master jester couldn't make stories out of it...

Since almost everything about his early years in Sydney has been touched, or concealed, by Hughes's own fancy, there is no prospect of beginning in any relevant way, except in the manner most relevant to a legendary figure—with his own legends. We may not know what is true, but what is really important about him is the myth.

***

His story commences heroically in Sydney with his arrival from Queensland on a coastal ship, having worked his way in the galley. His clothes are 'poor rags'; he has no shirt; he is wearing a flannel singlet, canvas trousers, a black alpaca coat and a broad-brimmed black felt hat—the kind of clothes that, in period revival, would now seem smart enough to be worn on a middle-class campus, but that then showed a man who was down on his luck. Like the pantomime Dick Whitington arriving in London, he carries the rest of his possessions (some neckties, some socks, some books) tied up in a handkerchief. He reaches socio-economic bottom (where he gathers some splendid material for after-dinner speeches) in the three nights he spends in a cave in the Sydney Domain with men who have given up trying, except for the crafty, abject talents of cadging, but he finds sustenance and the beginnings of self-definition as a restaurant kitchen man, offsider to chef and second cook, working seven days a week from five in the morning till nine at night. In a world where the three great verities are roast beef and yorkshire pudding, lamb and mint sauce, and curry and rice, his view of things is framed by the rectangle of the kitchen hatch, and what he can see of the botanical gardens and the harbour during the two hours he is occasionally given off on a Sunday afternoon.

Will Hughes might have spent the rest of his life moving from one restaurant kitchen to another, ending up an old windbag, telling tall tales as he peeled the spuds and washed the grease off the dishes. Later he was to tell the story of how, as a member of the New South Wales parliament in Macquarie Street, he met a former associate, now chief cook in a big city restaurant, with every Sunday off. When Hughes told him he was in a big place in Macquarie Street the chief cook didn't ask questions: he assumed Hughes was working in the kitchen.

From his time as a kitchen man he drew ingredients to give point to his view of political life. One of his later stories was how, in a kitchen he worked in, he began the morning by clearing a wooden trough of a layer of cockroaches and black beetles, studded here and there with mice, usually dead, and rats, usually alive; from underneath this filth he would then rescue the bread (partly scraps back from the tables, the rest stale loaves cut up in chunks) that had been left soaking overnight. And just as from a mess of faction and ambition the politician can produce new promise for humankind, out of this mess of wet bread and vermin the chef would produce the Princess Alexandria pudding, the date pudding, the raisin pudding and the plum pudding that kept the customers happy. One might even suspect, as one sometimes does with politicians, as they swivel, with agony or glee, between public hopes and private finagling, that Hughes made the details of the deceit of the Alexandria pudding even more revolting than they were.

The world of the kitchen provided Hughes with stories of reckless commitments and outrageous confidence tricks, also familiar to the world of politics. His master tale is of the fifteen shillings-a-week job he landed at the Golden Gate Hotel on Brickfield Hill, not long after he arrived in

Sydney. He passed himself off as a cook, although he knew nothing, apart from a bit of grilling and damper-making, about cooking. In mock-heroic style, he tells how on the Friday he maintains a front. Then comes his day of reckoning. The publican's wife orders stuffed breast of mutton and jam tart for Sunday dinner. 'Yes, ma'am,' he says. He doesn't know how to cook either. But he'll give it a go. For five pages of mock-heroics he embellishes his fiasco. By the end of his tale you can smell the charred mutton and the burned onion. When the brittle jam tart shatters under the knife, he gets the sack. Similar themes of commitment and improvisation were to run through his later political anecdotes, but the anecdote of the burned mutton and the hardened tart was a story that Hughes told against himself. The stories he was later to tell, of administrative follies and endangered votes, would always end with Hughes winning.

From such heroic shiftlessness we move him, as his luck changes, from near pauperdom to a more genteel poverty, into the world of the dark, gleaming linoleum floor and the lustrous aspidistra, the life of the terraces of boarding houses on the fringe of the inner city. Hughes lived in one of these, a semi-detached bed-and-breakfast place called Oleander Lodge, from the one brave oleander tree in its front garden. It was a house where the front door was always kept open, and the landlady could always find room for one more lodger. In the manner of such lodging houses, it was dominated by the bed. Rooms and the sleepout verandahs were so crowded with beds that the bathroom and the lavatory, 'down the back', were the only places where a lodger might be alone. One can imagine the queues forming, the looking out to see if the coast was clear with ownership of the bathroom signalled by continued singing and the fragile privacy of the dunny maintained by keeping a hand on the latch.

With no possibility of unobserved domestic life beyond these few minutes of isolation, the people of Oleander Lodge, in their daily comings together, had to make the best of each other. Imagine Hughes, the tale spinner, as one of the people keeping them together by defining existence in recognisable Dickensian caricature—a magsman impelled by his own itch to make life bigger and simpler than, in his confusion, he could find it in his own heart. He is no more able to stop his mouth opening and shutting than a dog can stop its leg itching, but by this need to keep talking he is able to help the lodgers see life as something simple, to which they might all belong. But imagine him also as very amusing, endearing in his audacity, keeping people on side by making them laugh, as, later, he will get a laugh out of Lloyd George or Clemenceau.

His one anecdote of success in battling to find a decent workplace is told not in the sardonic mood of *The Threepenny Opera,* but in the quietly persevering mood of Samuel Smiles's *Self Help;* its message is that men succeed only by their own efforts. The tale begins in a tricky, un-Smilesian way, when Hughes, although never having done such work before, cons a maker of 'colonial ovens' into giving him a job paying sixpence for every latch and set of hinges and hooks he forges. He waits outside the shop, on his first day, at ten to six in the morning, not knowing whether he can turn bars of iron into latches and hinges and hooks, a Napoleon committed to action, but not yet knowing where the action will lead. He describes how he cuts the bars, lays them on the forge, blows up the fire, shapes the hot iron, hammers a weld, and at the end of the day lays out a dozen hinges for his boss to admire. He has proved he can do it. But not quickly enough for the sixpences to add up to a living. He sticks at it. He works hard, day by day, from 6 a.m. to 6 p.m. The boss encourages him. Soon he is earning as much as six shillings a day. Comforted by success, shining in the eyes of the landlady, he found the reassurance, he later said, that a man can be captain of his soul.

***

Little is known of William Hughes, his father, a carpenter and joiner. William Hughes was a pillar of the Welsh Baptist Church at Moorfields in London, a deacon, 'always immaculately dressed' and with 'the manners of an old world gentleman'. In politics, he was a working class tory, a carpenter with an admiration for Disraeli, one of those millions of working men who, throughout Europe, were lending support to the new right-wing political parties with which the old rulers were summoning emergent democracy to their advantage. His job was in the House of Lords.

Hughes was born within walking distance of his father's workplace, at Pimlico, on 25 September 1862, of a mother who was a domestic servant before, at the age of thirty-seven, she married the House of Lords' carpenter. Her own family, the Morrises, were not working class, but small farmers running two adjoining farms on the Welsh side of the English border; they were Church of England people. William Morris Hughes was seven when his mother died and he spent most of the next five years with the Morrises—during schooltime with a Morris aunt in Llandudno, who ran an apartment house, and at holiday time with a Morris aunt on the farm on which his mother was born, where he was remembered as a lively, if fragile little boy, keen to get on, alert, likely to question things, always asking for reasons why. By his own account, although an only child robbed of a mother and passed from aunt to aunt (but perhaps petted and cossetted by them) these were the happiest years of his life.

When Hughes left London for Australia on 8 October 1884, he was not a restless odd jobs man. He was the son of a respectable skilled tradesman tory and a mother whose family ran farms and apartment houses; his future career was seen as that of a schoolmaster. Apprenticed for five years in London as a pupil teacher, Hughes was one of the thousands poised for the ascent to a lower middle class that was by then, along with its opposites, becoming one of the strong characteristics of an industrialisation that, in London, may have thrown up more dreams of respectability than it threw up of revolution. Imagine him a pupil teacher, at St. Stephen's' School, Westminster, a school for the London poor, built in revival gothic as a memorial to a philanthropist. At eight o'clock each morning he would arrive in the headmaster's office and study for an hour, before putting in the five hours teaching for which he was paid £10 a year when he began, and £25 a year five years later. Frequently he had night classes to attend and each year he had to sit for the school's quarterly exams and an annual exam run by the government. Since it was a church school, he attended lectures on church history on Saturdays, a young man learning the habits of a diligence intended to bring him a modest reward. Hughes's school inspector and examiner was Matthew Arnold, who warmed the confidence of pupils with mildness, and was benevolent towards Hughes, rewarding him with a volume of Shakespeare's collected works. According to Hughes, who knew him only as a school inspector not as a poet and critic trying to save culture from the philistines, Matthew Arnold encouraged him in the wide reading without which it was difficult for public men to make speeches in the nineteenth century when literary allusions were as necessary to oratory as politicians now find statistical tables. There would have been times when Hughes escaped the herdishness of Oleander Lodge by putting his nose into a book.

His grounding in the ordinariness of modest lower middle-class ambitions was to play no part in the jaunty style that, later, he lived out in himself. When he became a political leader he would never be able to reach into the ordinary household preoccupations of ordinary suburbanites. As a political leader he would never seem normal. He was to be a man of winter storms, sowing winds. Was this dark part of him, as he himself seemed to suggest, some throwback to the fearsome God of his fathers revealed in his childhood, Sunday after Sunday, as offering 'the eternal torments of hell to which sinners were doomed'? Whatever the occasions for it, his fundamentalist sense of horror, sustained by apocalyptic visions of a blood-drenched world, was to make him the most politically acclaimed of Australia's many prophets of disaster.

Immigrants frequently re-make their background when they come to a new country, so that they change themselves to something closer to what they would like to be. When Will Hughes left London he put his age back two years, and clung to this younger age for the rest of his life. And along with this fiction, he began to exaggerate his Welshness. His 're-making' of himself included a claim to have been born in Wales when, in fact, he was born in London, and a claim that he spoke more Welsh than English until he was about ten, coming to English as a foreign tongue, when, in fact, he lived in London until the age of seven, of Londonised parents and all the Welsh he could speak were a few phrases and setpiece sentences. Was Welshness something he had come to love (and there is no doubt that he did love the idea of it) and to identify himself with beyond his claim to it, because it gave some sense of coherence to a motherless child? Did it also give him a certain distinctiveness in the colonies that would not be found in a mere London cocksparrow? Did it even operate as a kind of justification for his oddities, helping him to get away with more, so that what was strange about him could seem to be not Hughes, but Welsh?

By the time he reached Oleander Lodge, Hughes had also gone through another kind of 're-making', not unusual in an immigrant, which could help add acceptable glamour to his strangeness. When he arrived in Brisbane in 1884 from London he picked up his ration vouchers at the immigration depot, tried, for a while, for an acceptable teaching job, then went bush. He was a 'new chum', an immigrant greenhorn, but ready to prove himself by gaining his 'colonial experience'. It was one of the great sustaining myths of the new world that a new society, colonial or ex-colonial, was a crucible, producing at its frontier new types of persons, uniquely self-reliant and individualistic. In the new world of Australia this crucible was to be found in the bush. (In Australia there was also a contrary sustaining myth, perhaps even greater, that the colonists' greatest source of pride was that they were, above all, true Britons.)

As he tells it, the saga of his labours in the bush begins with him working for a German pineapple grower outside Brisbane, or alternatively, as a tally clerk in the railway goods shed at Mitchell, 500 km west of Brisbane. Soon he joins a railway construction gang as a navvy. His first day is poignantly symbolic. It is blistering hot and black with flies; he reports to the foreman: they put a shovel in his hands. The pupil-teacher has joined the labouring classes! In fact, the shovel is too hard to manage so they put him on to breaking stones; his back aches, his hands blister; he vomits; he wakes 'as stiff as an old horse'. But he sticks at it. And on the job and in the bedroom he shares with half a dozen others, he also learns to curse. With buggers, bloodies, bastards and blithering blazes, Will Hughes has become an Australian.

The saga continues. He humps his bluey through the dry, hot, back country, picking up jobs where he can—boundary rider, striker to a blacksmith, pothole sinker, shed builder—then he sets off on a 1000 km tramp back to Brisbane. He is nearly four months on the track with his swag up, keeping near the waterholes, getting enough flour and tea at one station to last him out until he reaches the next. He arrives back in Brisbane sunburnt and broke, an even truer Australian.

Then he's off to join a mate in a factory at Maryborough, in the sugar country, where the islander kanakas are indentured to the plantations, and the Masters and Servants Act prevents a white man from leaving his job without his boss's permission. Hughes's mate takes a risk: he skips his job, although the boss says no. They run for it, concerned with keeping ahead of the police and the black trackers. With only enough flour for one meal, they find themselves lost in thick scrub matted with undergrowth and vines. After three days without food, and their swags and waterbags washed away, they could die. They reach the coast—but there is nothing to eat except oysters (and nothing to open the oysters with) and so little to drink that when they find a pool that isn't brackish they make a waterbag out of one of Hughes's trouser legs, and with this, and a few handfuls of winkles carried in a grubby handkerchief, they struggle on, fantasising about the great feed of chops and sausages and mashed potatoes that waits for them at the other end of the mirage. On the ninth day they find a timbercutter's house, and after three days' feasting on chops and damper with melon and lemon jam, they make it to Gympie, then take a paddle steamer to Brisbane.

Here the saga breaks up into its own contradictions. Hughes joins the Queensland navy during a Russian scare; alternatively, he joins the Queensland army and is sent to Thursday Island as part of a plan to foil the Russians; alternatively, he goes off droving to the Gulf of Carpentaria, or, alternatively, to Bourke. He falls ill at Bourke or, alternatively, Orange, and this makes him deaf; he treks to Sydney from Orange, or, alternatively, he works his way down from Brisbane to Sydney in a coastal steamer. The saga of his Sydney labours then begins, in which he is always the grand improviser, sustaining hope, or the perky moraliser, sweetening bitterness. With such a zealous and talented illusionist, the question of what is true and what is myth is only one question among others.

***

Number 16, Beattie Street, Balmain, is now a small electrical equipment factory, a flat, rectangular box of brick with a partly illegible sign outside. Beyond an abandoned iceworks and a couple of ruined houses, not much of the old Balmain is left around it. New families have moved in; there is only one old resident nearby. Most of the surviving terraces have been 'renovated' in waves of passing contemporary taste—1930s fibro flimsiness,

1950s liver-brick new affluence, 1960s clinker-brick trendiness.

In the 1890s, Number 16 was a small, weatherboard lock-up shop, squashed in between weatherboard houses, its iron-roofed verandah stretching over the pavement on to three wooden posts. It was here, in 1891, that Will Hughes and his wife, perhaps using money of his wife's, set up a small mixed business, so small that they both had to do other work. His wife (who had given birth to a son in 1887 and a daughter in 1888 and was to give birth to another daughter in 1892) took in washing; and Hughes further extended his repertoire of odd jobs, amongst other things walking from door to door offering to mend umbrellas. His reminiscences about jobs now altogether abandon the Smilesian mode and become wholly sardonic and Brechtian, boasting of an improvisor's deceit. He boasts of how, walking down a street, he notices some loose tiles on a building; he knocks on a door, meets the owner and says he is an expert tiler, fresh from 'Home'. Another boast tells how he passes himself off as a locksmith and pretends to make a new key for a safe of which the old key has been lost, but all he has really done is to find the old key—and take money for it. In the shop itself they sell general knick-knacks and reading matter—penny dreadfuls, secondhand books, and political books and pamphlets.

At one end of Beattie Street, in sight of Number 16, is Loyalty Square, a wide crossroads. In the centre of Loyalty Square there is now a World War I memorial, in decay. It is sustained with age, a few pieces have crumbled off. Some of its lettering is defaced—but the main words still stick out. One on each of the four sides of the plinth, there they are: LIBERTY...PEACE...HONOUR...EMPIRE.

These are keywords in the grand rhetoric for which Hughes is remembered. But the political books and pamphlets he and his wife sold in the shop in Beattie Street were concerned with a different range of words: REFORM...EQUALITY...REASON... THE PEOPLE. Will Hughes was more than a story teller and a con-man. The tough, self-justifying, long-winded glorying in a scrupulous lack of scruple may have made it easier for him to bear the failure of existence to match the ideals humans can hold for it—perhaps as he got older it was almost all that was left of him—but when he was younger it may also have provided a shelter from the surrounding philistinism that Matthew Arnold wrote about, and may even have spoken of to the young pupil-teacher. It may have allowed the more sensitive sides of Hughes some possibility of a continued, if fugitive, existence. In a contemporary photograph the upper lip is poised for talk; but the equally determined eyes could be those of an intelligent, self-taught working class boy who wanted to get on with his reading.

Through his reading, and perhaps from other ways, by the time he was selling political books in his shop Hughes had become a *radical*. He believed that he understood deeply into events and that from what he knew it was easy to find ways to change what was happening. We don't know how he became a radical, but at that time the whole possible range of human motivation could lead Europeans to radicalism. (Equally, it could lead them to conservatism.) Human existence had been so enormously shaken by the triumph of the machines and of the new factories and mechanised communication networks that, whether they liked it or not, or knew it or not, every European was, in effect, on one side or the other. What matters is not how Hughes became a radical, but what kind of radical it was that he later turned into.

From what we know of the books in Hughes's shop and the kind of names thrown around in his talking and reminiscing, there were two main strains in the radicalism of Number 16, Beattie Street. The spirit of reason and the spirit of progress were nurtured in the little weatherboard lock-up shop run by a laundress and her odd-jobs-man husband, in the makeshift suburb of workmen's cottages and small factories running down the side of the hill to Blackwattle Bay. The radicalism of reason stripped away old Christian beliefs and replaced them with a new language. The radicalism of progress believed that the great human disasters and inequalities accompanying the new machines could be easily transformed into triumphs for the common people.

In the places where Hughes was doing his reading and talking, the voice of reason was found in the works of Herbert Spencer, a former English railway engineer who had retired to an ascetic boarding-house life so that he could write big books explaining everything. He saw evolution as the simple explanation of matters as diverse as the formation of the earth, the growth of an embryo, the development of a species or the formation of social institutions, and, after boldly drawing a series of metaphors from animals' bodies and applying them to human societies, he offered rationalist science as a cure for human disappointments. Wherever he went in his long, changeable life, Hughes always carried with him some of this belief in progress through rationality, even if he would sometimes defend it by methods that were spectacularly irrational.

The language of reason also seemed to mean for Hughes the language of scientific secularism. Darwinism, in Hughes's words, *had shaken the Christian world to its foundations*. Hughes was a materialist, and he saw the materialists as holding *the stage of science and philosophy...Huxley, Tyndall, Mill, Spencer were names to conjure with, Kant and Schopenhauer were outmoded. The indestructible atom was firmly enshrined in the physicists' conception of matter which, with force, not less material than matter itself explained everything—even life and consciousness. Man had been reminded that, far from being a little lower than the angels, he was in sober fact only a few generations ahead of the reptile and the ape.*

For this dilemma of lost Christian faith Hughes sold answers in his shop, in books about the new secular religions and the heaven on earth they promised. One of them, *Looking Backward,* had been a world best-seller since it came out in 1888, making its author, the American journalist Edward Bellamy, one of the prophets of his time. In this utopian romance, set in Boston in the year 2000, the tale is told of how the evils of capitalism were swept away by the National Party, a party that destroyed the old class barriers so quickly that people became rational in one generation. Impelled by the new religion of Solidarity, in a co-operative commonwealth in which the real meaning of life lay in working for the common good, they scorned personal possessions, preferring public goods—grand buildings, landscaped gardens, sculptures, splendidly marbled public dining halls. Money had ceased to exist; from birth all the people were joint stockholders in the one Great Monopoly that controlled all production. Most of the political and administrative aspects of the state had dissolved: with government simply a question of production, depending on devotion and self service, what was there left to make laws about?

In his shop, beside a copy of *Looking Backward,* there might lie a copy of *News from Nowhere* by the English poet-craftsman, William Morris, which was written to provide an anarchist's answer to Bellamy's Great Monopoly. It is set in London in the twenty-second century, in a green and pleasant land of craftsmen wearing medieval-revival dress who have abolished factories. With its exploitation and its alienating division of labour, capitalism has gone, leaving people free to be instinctively co-operative and happy; since goods are produced purely for the joy of working, salaries and money are unnecessary. And since there is no property to protect, there is no government. Parliament House (renamed the Dung Market) has become a storing place for fertiliser. With no idle rich to breed them there are no criminals and therefore no law courts and no police. With equality of condition for the sexes, there is no marriage; people live together freely. There are no schools; children learn by doing and receive formal education only when they want it.

In Loyalty Square there was a big open air meeting each Sunday night, devoted to the sharing of radical opinion.

In Hughes's shop itself, any night of the week, there could be meetings of people who wanted to make a better world. The shop was becoming both an informal school and an informal debating society. Sometimes, with fellow workmen, Hughes might be quietly sitting there, working on a repair as the others talked; he was only a 'wisp of a fellow who, if he was sold by the pound weight wouldn't bring very much', but when 'he began to fidget, chew nervously and tense himself' and then 'toss his work aside, spring to his feet and launch his attack', there would come out of him the harsh voice and the sharply chopped logic that could make him seem the biggest man in Balmain.

He was learning how to make speeches. Speech-making, preferably in the grand style, was an essential skill in the political life of the late nineteenth century, when being able to hold a crowd and gain its applause was one of the tests of statemanship and something with which some statesmen satisfied themselves, attempting very little else. Along with reading himself into an education, learning the rules of oratory was a way in which a young worker might enter the Political classes, and by now Hughes was teaching himself to speak in public. One might imagine three scenes:

...A little figure stands alone in the Beattie Street shop, declaiming to the wooden walls, trying out an opening piece, or a special rhetorical flourish, or a stirring conclusion. In the silence of the empty shop, when he finishes his speech, he imagines what it would be like to be hearing loud and prolonged applause. Then he tries it again, this time standing in front of a long mirror, moving his hands this way, that way, to see what looks best. But what he is practising is not mob oratory. He is giving himself an elocution lesson.

...The second scene is an eisteddfod. Imagine a crowded hall, a stage decorated with potted palms for the impromptu speeches contest. Hughes, self-taught in elocution, if with help from some friends, draws 'Myself' as the subject on which he must give his impromptu. He stands and declaims, carefully matching gesture with word, then he sits and listens to the others. The judges make their comments and announce him the winner.

...Through scenes of Hughes speaking from notes in discussions at the Sydney school of arts, or throttling opponents with words in suburban debating societies, come to another scene of success: his first street corner meeting. He stands on his 'spruiking box' with lamp above it and shouts out what he thinks. The scene is repeated: every Saturday night some boys help him carry the lamp and the little platform along Beattie Street into Darling Street, and he gives his message. The platform itself becomes as necessary to him and as familiar on his lonely journey as a faithful horse.

The great message for humankind Hughes was proclaiming from Darling Street, Balmain, was the infallible merit of the 'single tax', to some people as universal a remedy for the social ills of humanity as the pills, potions and electric belts proclaimed in the newspaper advertisements as cure-alls for the human body. Hughes had found a path to utopia in the prophecies of the United States journalist, Henry George. The single tax, a tax equal to the unimproved rental value of all land, *would extirpate land monopoly, the principal evil of society, raise wages, abolish pauperdom, increase the earning power of capital, provide full employment for all who wanted it, afford free scope to human powers, lessen crime, elevate morals and taste and intelligence, purify government and carry civilisation to yet greater heights.* When Henry George himself arrived in Sydney in 1890, Hughes and his friends heard all this from the prophet's own mouth: George was welcomed at a public banquet in the Town Hall presided over by the lord mayor and given a free pass on the New South Wales government railways; he spent three months stumping the colonies expounding this new secular religion to crowded meetings and when he went he left behind him converts who, for a season, fervently carried on his cause. In 1891 Hughes took on his first public office: he became president of the Balmain Single Tax League.

And he wrote his first letter to the editor, an act that in someone who later becomes a public figure, might be celebrated, as much as in more religious days were memories of a first communion. Hughes's first letter-to-the-editor was published in a weekly threepenny paper called the *Democrat* (a single tax paper which for a while carried the slogan *Liberty. Justice. Fraternity.*) on 5 December 1891, just before it folded. Since it is the only early stage of his initiation that survives exactly as it happened without being mythologised, or suppressed, we should treat it with the respect of a rare inscription preserved in a national archeological museum.

In his letter Hughes was defending state socialism from attacks made on it in an earlier article, which had said that state socialism would need force to compel acceptance. He begins both with stagey arrogance (*under cover of elaborate terminology,... a profusion of platitudes...much that is inaccurate and illogical*) and then with copybook obsequiousness (*I must crave your permission to trespass so far on your valuable space as will enable me to reply to him*). However the rest is argued with straightforward seriousness.

He points out that *since socialism could not exist until the people as a whole were convinced of its superiority, it was likely to be less coercive than other systems. It would do much to expand and accentuate the individuality of the members of the community by assisting them to find their proper spheres, and as far as it removed from the shoulders of the unit the necessity of thinking and planning as to how he should supply himself with the necessaries of life— a process of thought which, so far from being conducive to the retention or development of individuality, tended rather to reduce all men to one pattern—it would, in a much greater degree, have the effect of bringing out all that was best and noblest in the man.*

At the end, he goes back to the attack. The modern world is not so much OVERgoverned as MIS-*governed. Socialism sought to supersede the anarchy which existed today in modes of distribution and production by a system which would give the greatest return with the minimum of regulation. Just as an undisciplined body of men, having many commanders, could be readily overcome by an organised body vastly inferior in numbers, which had its actions directed by* ONE *authority, wielding its powers intelligently and constantly; so the productive forces of Society would be indefinitely increased in efficiency, by the National System of Industrialism, which it was the office of Socialism to establish.*

It is now at the time that Hughes began seeing himself as a single-taxer determined to break the land monopoly, that he took off as an orator. After his Saturday night in Darling Street, with his spruiking box and lamp, he would go on Sunday afternoon to the Domain, the greatest of the city's popular forums, where people would take the air and if they were newcomers shop around to decide which speaker to listen to or, perhaps, heckle; if they were regulars, they might join one of the discussion groups that gathered around some of the platforms and then have their go at socialism or the single tax or Darwinism or philosophy, or the political issues of the day. Among them, 'his hard voice laying down the law in a clear emphatic manner', his speech illustrated by quotations from his favourite writers, is Hughes, a little man with bright brown eyes, his head bent to one side as he corrects every error and proclaims every truth. His arms move nervously. Every few minutes he brings up two fingers of his right hand, shakes them, then slaps them down on his left.

At night all the spruiking boxes are put away and Hughes goes up some badly lit stairs to the meeting hall in 'Leigh House' in Brickfield Hill, the club rooms of the Australian Socialist League, which has links with the Second International in a dozen European countries. Sometimes the lecturing is about coin-collecting, or the mysteries of the universe, or idealist philosophy, but more often than not speakers from a variety of secular religions profess a faith that poverty can be abolished and general happiness secured. Although the speakers are united in this common purpose, like the Christians before them they are divided about which way to get there; in particular some of them are divided about which sacred texts to invoke and those who accept the same text are likely to be divided on how to interpret it. But Sunday by Sunday they profess their belief in the possibility of salvation through politics.

By joining this small group seeking salvation from an upstairs room in George Street, Hughes was joining a movement made up of similar groups throughout the European countries, all of them thrown up by the processes that followed the invention of the machine; and by now some of them were imagining that salvation from the evil effects of the machine, or of wage earning generally, might come from the very 'working class' that the machines had created, beginning with those wretches, three-quarters women and children, who, in the cotton mills of Lancashire, came together to suffer a new kind of enslavement, not previously known to humankind, in which, as if themselves made of metal and wood, they became appendages of the recently invented 'mechanical tools'. The first factory proletariat, a proletariat of barefooted women and men, and children in rags, thin and pale, dehumanised, like animals on a treadmill, with little to their lives beyond toil and sleep, had produced the beginnings of a new way for humans to see themselves collectively. This was the awareness, strong and bright amongst some, weak and shadowy amongst others—and now being discussed in some of the pubs or cottages or verandahs of Balmain—of being a *worker*, a *toiler*, seen as collectively suffering, but with their own valid lifestyles, their own sense of honour and their own sense of legitimate ambitions. Some of the speakers in Loyalty Square, or Darling Street, or the Domain saw this class as uniquely able to offer release from its predicament; a few saw them as the sole bearers of humanity's light for the future. When Hughes walked up the stairs in Leigh House, in a colony where most factories were still small, he might be going to a meeting in which a speaker would present the whole colony as a kind of factory, with an 'employer class' in control, running not only their own businesses and farms and mines, but coming together in trusts and combines, and through their agents controlling members of parliament, judges, government officials. In Leigh House, against the employer class all wage earners could seem to have a common interest. Occasionally there was a monster meeting or a long procession that could seem to give substance to these feelings of unity. Perhaps something might happen.

This was a new language for Hughes to learn. In the 1880s when 'the loyal toast' was proposed at the annual dinners of the Trades and Labor Council in the presence of the premier and, once or twice, the governor, speakers at intercolonial trades union congresses could speak of strikes as a *relic of a barbaric age*, of *the reciprocal obligations between workers and their social superiors* and of *the need for an indissoluble solidarity of interest uniting employer and employee, one belonging to the other as the limbs to the hand*. But now, after the failure of the strikes of 1888, 1890, 1891 and 1892 class difference in Sydney was being defined more frequently and more bitterly.

Hughes was able to read about the drama of these great strikes in which, by their use of the police with rifles and bayonets and of the army at times with artillery, and by arrests and imprisonments, the colonial governments showed that whatever might have happened at Labor Council annual dinners, at a time of confrontation governments saw the interests of the State as the interests of the employers. Two particular acts of political theatre cast images of desperation. In Melbourne a British colonel ordered the men of the Mounted Rifles: 'If the order is given to fire don't let me see any rifle pointed in the air; fire low and lay them out so that the duty will not have to be performed again'. And at Broken Hill mounted police and foot police with fixed bayonets surrounded a building and arrested five members of the strike committee, put them into leg-irons and charged them with criminal conspiracy.

The unions had their supporters. They would demonstrate their solidarity in meetings of up to 50,000 and in processions of up to 2500 km. The Chief Justice of Victoria, George Higinbotham, paid £50 to their strike fund and Henry Lawson wrote them *Freedom on the Wallaby*, which would later become essential in the thin repertoire of Australian revolutionism:

> But Freedom's on the Wallaby,
> She'll knock the tyrants silly.
> She's going to light another fire
> And boil another billy.
> We'll make the tyrants feel the sting
> Of those that they would throttle;
> They needn't say the fault is ours
> If blood should stain the wattle.

But each time, in 1888, 1890, 1891, 1892, the unions gave in. All the unions were weakened. Some collapsed. It was a defeat most of their leaders had never imagined.

It could now seem true to many people, as the secretary of the General Labourers' Union put it, *the old cry, 'Defence not defiance', must give place to self-help, mutual help, and active organised attack upon the system that makes the many dependent on the few for the right to exist. By the exercise of political power in our hands we can remodel our laws until Law and Order shall deserve respect, be voluntarily obeyed, and cease to be terms conveying to our minds the idea of tyranny and injustice.* Will Hughes became one of them. He abandoned the single taxers, joined the Australian Socialist League and in December 1891 helped form a branch of the Socialist League at Balmain. For several years after that (although later he would deny it) he regularly called himself a socialist, and regretted that in the labour movement there were those who didn't see themselves in the same way.

A socialist, but not a revolutionary. Although 'Leigh House' could be scorned by the more adventurous as a place where *frock-coated and white-collared gents babbled in utopian, wordy warfare of what they did not feel,* some of those who spoke there agreed with William Morris that there would necessarily be violence before change would occur and a few saw Karl Marx as the writer who really understood the laws that underlay society. But what they were likely to mean by being socialists was not that they were revolutionaries but that Henry George, in seeking the destruction of land monopoly, did not go far enough; what was needed was the nationalisation of the whole means of production. Most of those who, in Hughes's words, *saw the vision splendid and, uplifted by an abiding faith, marched shoulder to shoulder, men and women of diverse creeds united by a great and holy purpose, their ideals a fulfilment of the scriptures,* did not even think of 'unconstitutional' struggle; all that was needed was to put into parliament a political party of their own.

This could be true even of those who demanded a change in the whole social system. They could say: *The present industrial system, commonly called the competitive system, is destructive, pernicious, and altogether evil, and must be replaced by a social system which will not leave it in the power of one man to take advantage of the necessities or disabilities of another.* Yet even the people who drafted this resolution, calling for a change in the system, saw as the means of getting it nothing more ambitious than a 'People's Parliament', by which they meant nothing more than universal suffrage, one-man-one-vote, annual parliaments and abolition of upper house or governors' vetoes. Their aims were revolutionary but their methods were constitutional.

The time when Hughes moved from the Balmain Single Tax League to the Balmain Socialist League was one of groupings and re-groupings between parliamentary factions, with a few independents pirouetting here and there. There were no party machines and, usually, no broad election issues. In most electorates 'appropriate attention to the needs of the district' was enough, perhaps with a bit of local spice added by the struggle between Catholics and masons, or publicans and temperance societies, or protectionists and freetraders. Political parties began to form in New South Wales at much the same time, and for much the same reasons as they did throughout the European nations: with the new concepts of mass participation in politics, and the new use of mass support for political power, politics wasn't possible without them.

In this context it seems quite natural that (at the time when Hughes was still a single taxer) the Trades and Labor Council formed the Labor Electoral League to fight the 1891 elections. Members of parliament were now paid, so Labor members could support themselves in parliament. In any case the unions had become so weak that perhaps parliament seemed the only place to go. The main division, insofar as people actually saw it, was on expectations about what a Labor Party might do. Some saw ahead little more than that Labor MPs would be a minority, representing union interests: *Once let Labour be adequately represented in the legislature and the cause of unionism is assured. Laws can be framed in support of trade unionism.* Others imagined the Labor men gaining a majority and working for rapid change. *The worker must set about the work of reform where it seems that reform can alone be obtained, and that is in parliament. Then, and only then, can we begin to restore to the people the land of which they have been plundered, to absorb the monopolies which society at large has helped to create, and to ensure to every man, by the opportunity of fairly remunerated labour, a share in those things that make life worth living.*

In 16 Beattie Street, change seemed easy. The idea of 'capitalism' was still a novelty. Ideas like 'trust', 'ring' and 'combine' were even more new. There was confidence that institutions that seemed to have come so quickly might equally quickly be destroyed. Just as the early Christians waited expectantly for an early second coming in which human affairs would be settled forever, many people who followed moderate paths could nevertheless believe in 'socialism in our time', to be achieved quickly, by acts of parliament. For Hughes the socialist, the achievement of socialism by act of parliament was what he spoke about and wrote about, although the non-socialist majority in the Labor League expected something less.

In August 1893, Hughes became a Labor Party organiser. An advertisement appeared in the *Worker* for 'Political Organisers, to visit all Shearing Sheds, Mining Districts, Townships, and centres of Population in the Young, Grenfell, Forbes, Wellington, Bogan, Carcoar, Burrowa, Orange, Molong and portions of other electorates'. The advertisement had been put there by the Trades Council in Young, a wool town that had grown out of the old gold diggings of Lambing Flat and that had become a centre of the two great bush unions whose leaders, remembering the dash and improvisation that had formed their own remarkable organisations of nomadic workmen, were ready to repeat the trick by whipping up Labor Electoral Leagues in country areas to fight the next election.

As one of the men who got a job, Hughes's task was to organise local leagues in three electorates and to enrol members at the rate of four shillings a head. It was a time when political parties were so novel that there were no recognised techniques about how to start them, or how to run them. In fact the NSW Labor Electoral League already had a sense of fiasco. It had begun well, with the exhilarating success of the 1891 election in which, with practically no organisation behind them, 35 Labor candidates had won seats in a parliament of 141 members; then after their first meeting together as a caucus, one member at once split off and seven others went as soon as they faced their first difficult vote in the house; faced with another difficult vote the remaining members argued with each other for ten days, some of it publicly, then nine others dropped out. Even more ludicrously, in 1892 when the Labor member for Broken Hill moved censure of the government for its suppression of the strike, four Labor men voted with the government. The language of Australian politics extended to include the phrase 'Labor rat'.

Hughes's legendary tales of himself at this time have him prominent in both union affairs and party affairs, but there is no trace of his name in the weekly newspapers in which these things were argued out, nor any trace of him attending, as a delegate, the meetings where the Labor men counted their disasters and began to ask themselves to whom were the Labor members of parliament to be responsible, and what were they there for. In the year Hughes became an organiser, the League's new platform suggested that the great causes of mankind were, in this order: the land tax, mining rights for prospectors, abolition of the upper house, introduction of the referendum, local government on a democratic basis, the eight-hour day, and establishment of a state bank.

Off Hughes went into the central west, where only fifty or sixty years before, the squatters had walked into the wilderness with their sheep and their horses and their bullock drays and their convict or ex-convict shepherds, and stolen their 'runs' from the blacks. Several decades later a second generation of gamblers, this time after gold, had raided the hillsides and gullies and plains, turned the earth over, tunnelled into it, throwing up streets of duckboards and calico tents, and then hurried on. A third gamblers' rush began: in one of the nineteenth century's first land reform movements small farmers, dreaming of a decent independence, staked claims out of the squatters' sheep walks, set up their bark humpies, chopped down trees, dug into the earth and were frequently foreclosed by moneylenders.

All three invasions had thrown up characteristic types, with whom Hughes had to deal. The squatters, now in large, and sometimes stately, houses, lived a life apart, in which it could seem appropriate to kick a skinny little agitator like Hughes off their properties; but also on their properties were the shearers' quarters, where itinerant workmen, union-organised and now being glamorised as mythically Australian, had made the wool shearing shed one of the symbols of Australian radicalism; they provided one of Hughes's easiest markets. Some of the gold diggings were now only scoured earth and heaped-up muck, or they had grown into towns that had found other purposes, but they had thrown up memories of 'the digger' and then 'the miner' as another fighter for a better world and wherever minefields survived Hughes had another radical audience. Some of the small farmers, the 'cockies', still feeling badly served in what was by now a second generation of farm failures might see in this new party a unique understanding of what was wrong with their treatment, and some of them might also give Hughes a hand. In the towns and smaller settlements that grew out of these economic activities there were types of people—small gentry, small bosses, clerks, and those who admired them, who might see Hughes as just another down-at-heel itinerant to hunt out of town, but in the places which the railway had reached there were the railwaymen, and in all the settlements there were those who saw themselves distinctively as 'toilers', and might help organise his meetings.

In the bush generally there was an affected equality of manner, supported by legends of 'mateship', a yearning for recognition of common frailties, but imported political creeds had no answer to such native aspirations. It was not a language that Hughes, who had been in Australia less than nine years, had learned to speak. Of the Labor members of parliament, two-thirds were immigrants. And even if they had found a more Australian form of talking about their parties, how could they have used it? 'Mateship' might be the language of ordinary life, but how could it be the language of Parliament, or of public ceremony?

Hughes spent seven months and may have travelled as

much as 5000 km organising branches and enrolling members in the central west—Imagine him, sometimes on a bicycle, sometimes on a borrowed horse, sometimes simply walking, with his receipt book and his party literature in his swag, moving on to the next town. He has already made a forward contact and the contact has hired a hall and put out posters advertising a 'Monster Meeting', respectfully adding 'God Save the Queen!' After he arrives Hughes speaks to local supporters; they tick off names and wonder how big the crowd will be; Hughes writes out receipts for any who have already been enrolled, someone walks up and down the main street ringing the bell and proclaiming that the meeting starts at eight; Hughes and the supporters get there early to see who turns up. Then, whether the hall is full, or half full, or almost empty, the ritual begins: after being introduced by the local identity, Hughes makes his speech, urging people to join the Labor Electoral League, a speech he is to make more than a hundred times in his seven months of organising. At the end, he listens to the vote of thanks, then gets out his receipt book. In the follow-up over the next week or so, if it is a good town he may enrol a hundred new members or more, and school them in keeping minutes, making reports, preparing for elections. In a bad town he may speak to a row or two of people in a school of arts where otherwise all the chairs are empty. There is no response to anything he says. No questions. No vote of thanks. His audience just gets up and silently goes home.

He is poor. He is ordered out of a shearing shed. The landlady of a hotel refuses to serve him a meal or put him up. A forward contact disappears. Posters are not distributed. The chairman at one of his meetings eats the bag of peaches that were to have been his supper. He gives a blacksmith a membership ticket as payment for shoeing a horse. He wears his overcoat at meetings because the seat is worn out of his trousers...Now pull the camera back to get a wider view. This little man cycling along the red dust roads through a disastrously over-stocked and now drought-stricken landscape beyond the edge of which, on the great western plains, much of the land will never recover, is only one of tens of thousands of people travelling through the countrysides and the towns of the European nations, setting up the local branches of the new kinds of mass political parties that are to become the unique units of political contact.

Now imagine him back home from one of his organising trips. It is March, 1894, and he is in town for the Labor Electoral League's third annual conference, to which, as a country organiser he has been appointed a delegate. Here is Will Hughes, aged 31, in his flimsy wooden house with a seven-year-old son, a six-year-old daughter and a two-year-old daughter. Still passing from one job to the next, with nothing permanent in sight, he dresses with the perky neatness of a man who knows how to hide the hole in the seat of his pants and how to act as if he has more than one shirt. He is not in Sydney often, and when he is, he might be out speaking on street corners or in the Domain, or giving a lecture at Leigh House, or taking part in a debate at the School of Arts. His wife is pregnant again, about to have her fourth baby. Their relationship is on the way down.

All around him is the city in which, by the standards of those who run it, he is a man of straw. Yet when he looks at the wharves and shipyards, the little factories, the timber yards and chemical works of Balmain, and then across the harbour to the banks and warehouses, the retail emporiums, the ministries and government departments, he can see all this as in the grip of masters who can be overthrown, or at least forced to make room for him and his brothers. All he needs is the strength of the people who laugh at the jokes about the rich he makes at street meetings, and who applaud the promises of a better future he makes in the Domain. Pull the camera back, get a wider view and see him as only one among the tens of thousands of people in the labour movements of the European nations who now believe that if they and their brothers and sisters hold together they will overthrow the older order, by revolt or reform, walk into the palaces of power and renew the world. They are a generation doomed to an ironic success. Some of them will sit in the masters' chairs. But some will still have masters sitting beside them.

Now imagine Hughes going to the annual conference of the Labor Electoral League on the morning of March 2. This time he is a member of the central executive committee probably because he has been playing a second, if strong, fiddle to his friend William Arthur Holman. Holman is an immigrant like Hughes; he is as slender as Hughes, but elegantly so, rather than, like Hughes, merely skinny; and as talkative, but mellifluously, rather than raucously. In the schools of arts debates, at night classes and literary societies and in his reading at the public library, and even as one of the participants in all the projections of a better world that went on at the Beattie Street shop, he has already shown a middle-class assuredness, although he works with his hands—as a cabinet-maker. When he was a lad, as the son of a successful actor, and as a prize winner at school, he was growing up with lower middle-class expectations of a middle-class career; but his father went down in the world, and Holman was apprenticed. He is nine years younger than Hughes, but he has already hit top attention in the small world of the labour movement, both as ideologue and as fixer. Five and a half months ago this twenty-two-year-old cabinet-maker began a series of lectures on economics at Leigh House. He drew on Ruskin, Jevons, George, Ricardo, Spencer, the Austrian economist Bohm-Bawerk and Karl Marx ('calm and unimpassioned...one of the simplest and clearest of writers') and set people talking about him both as a brilliant and compassionate young man, and as an arrogant and disruptive young puppy. Four months ago, at a Labor unity conference, he was the central executive committee's young tough; despite complaints about stacking and use of the gag, it was he who got through the conference a resolution that demanded that all Labor MPs should pledge themselves not only to vote in parliament to support the party's platform, but, on certain key issues, to vote as a majority of their caucus decided.

Now imagine a meeting at the conference between these two ambitious young Londoners—the twenty-two-year-old and his thirty-one-year-old odd-jobs-man offsider. Both neatly dressed, both winners of blue ribbons in elocution contests. Imagine them putting their heads together, talking softly, keeping an eye out for passers-by—looking up, smiling at friends, smiling at enemies, cracking jokes. Then they pull their heads down again. What they want to do is to put the Labor MPs in their place, as servants of the movement, by confirming the unity conference resolution demanding loyalty to caucus decisions. They know what their arguments are going to be in the coming weeks. Holman will say that *it was the workers themselves, gathered in a conference like this, who should decide what the labour movement was to be—not just a few men chosen from the ranks of the workers and put into parliament, in most cases by pure luck, who then imagined they could become the dictators of the whole labour movement.* Hughes has a metaphor ready: *The movement had picked these men up, breathed the breath of political life into their carcases and brought them into being. The movement could as easily prick the bubble and these men would collapse into nothingness.*

Imagine that they nod to each other, and move away. In the manner of politics they are acting with the sense of righteousness and the itch of ambition of new men, who, by displaying their greater zeal and their greater purity, can distinguish themselves from those who have been there before them. A generation later, as premier and prime minister, these two zealots of party loyalty will be expelled from the party on those very questions of party disloyalty which they are now condemning in others.

Out of the conference came two Labor parties, each declaring the other bogus, each preparing to destroy the other in the elections. The fight moved to the Domain and to the radical weeklies. Since these were inclined to support the party of the MPs rather than the Solidarity Labor Party that had come out of the conference, what Holman and Hughes and other central executive committee supporters needed was a weekly of their own. It was a time when a weekly newspaper could be started, and published for at least a few issues, at little more than the price of one or two personal bankruptcies. An immigrant stone mason, A. G. Yewen, a London socialist and a friend of William Morris, was ready to risk the bankruptcy: he sold or mortgaged everything he had to found *New Order*, a radical weekly, which was to support the Solidarity Party and advocate socialism. One of the founders of the Australian Socialist League became a manager; the socialists Holman and Hughes were to be two of its writers.

In his reminiscences Hughes made yet another merry Dickensian tale out of the hired typewriters, the packing cases used instead of furniture, the flurries of unpaid bills, the evasions of the bailiffs, the kindnesses of tradesmen in giving them something to eat, even if it was only corned beef, wine and damaged apples, the libel actions, but for Yewen it was an about turn in his whole life: after seventeen issues *New Order* collapsed. For those seventeen issues, however, *New Order* came out with a confident face, rosy with radicalism.

With *New Order* each week demonstrating the merits of socialism and the follies and evils of 'Bogus Labor', 'the traitor interest' and 'the Labor rats', Hughes and Holman got to work in their other arena of propaganda—the public forums of the Domain. At the end of April Hughes addressed a crowd of 5,000; the next week, at a meeting in which one of the leaders of 'Bogus Labor' moved a motion in support of his side, Holman, with Hughes seconding, came in, cut the ground away from their opponents by moving a Solidarity amendment—and again won the crowd, again reckoned at 5,000. The next Sunday was May Day and since the Second International had recently suggested that May Day should be dedicated to the labor movement, the large crowd that had again gathered in the Domain was this time turned into a May Day rally; the rhetoric rolled, asserting the need for economic freedom and the right of all men to life, liberty and the pursuit of happiness. When it was Hughes's turn, he moved that the meeting *deplore the existence of the privileged class, and reaffirm the fundamental declaration that private property in the natural sources of production and in the instruments of labour was the obvious cause of all economic servitude*. Carried with ringing cheers. In the evening a big roll-up at 'Leigh House' listened to vocal and instrumental music, followed by speeches supporting another socialist resolution; Hughes's speech, with the mixture of humour and sarcasm people now expected, made the audience laugh and clap. The evening concluded with a great expression of *good heartedness and fixedness of purpose for better conditions for the toilers of New South Wales and other lands*. At the beginning of the next month, Hughes was selected as the Solidarity Labor Party candidate for the electorate of Lang.

There were only 2,115 voters registered in Lang. Its whole length could be walked in half an hour and its breadth could be crossed in a few minutes. One boundary was George Street, a confidently defined thoroughfare in a city that was never planned with the precise imperial geometry of most other Australian towns, on the other side were the irregularities of the wharves and sheds of Darling Harbour; running down the centre was a street of produce stores and warehouses; in between were the courts and lanes of workmen's cottages, rundown, tightly packed, where wharf labourers, storemen, carters and other toilers lived. Apart from the shabby gentility of a boarding house district around Wynyard Square and a brothel area near the town hall, this was the kind of area (matched in the Australian colonies only by the pit villages and minefield towns) in which, throughout the European nations, the awareness of being 'a worker' was most likely to arise: it was workplace and dwelling place all together, with some of the sense of community of a village.

However, they were not factory workers in Lang; they looked for their living to the coastal waters over which ships moved produce between the ports of the colonies and like those workers further along the waterfront who worked on the wharves where the deep sea ships went out, it was possible that more important to them than the question of class was the question of whether trade should be free, or whether taxes should be imposed on imported goods to 'protect' local factories and encourage new factories to develop. As the infant party system was taking form in New South Wales it was not on the question of 'Capital' versus 'Labour' that humankind was seen to be most seriously divided, but on the 'fiscal issues' of 'Protectionists' versus 'Freetraders'.

Hughes was lucky. His 'Bogus Labor' opponent, J. D. Fitzgerald, an old hand in the labour movement who had won a seat in parliament in 1891 and was now looking for another one, was not only a 'Labor rat' who had voted in support of the Government that gaoled the Broken Hill strike leaders; he was also a protectionist. As the candidates formed their working committees and sub-committees, and arranged their fund-raising smoke concerts and their canvassing teams to knock on doors and visit workplaces, the candidate Hughes had to beat seemed to be not the candidate of 'the old Labor Party' but Alderman John Taylor, a local timber merchant, who stood on a straight Freetrade platform. In this little district of workmen's cottages and boarding houses in a colonial seaport a struggle was going on to draw new political battlelines to replace the old. A similar struggle—to make the issue of class the decisive issue in human conflict—was going on in every other European country.

Hughes was the first of the candidates to form his working committee and arrange his smoke concert. And he was the first to start spruiking. The four years of talk in the Beattie Street shop, and all the town hall elocution contests, schools of arts debates, Leigh House lectures, streetcorner oratory, country campaigning and preaching in the Domain—all that opening and shutting of the lips, and all those wavings of the hands—had now led to his participation in one of the most significant rituals in modern life: an election campaign, with its ceremonies of affirmation of social values and legitimisation of political masters.

The long columns of small type in the newspapers recorded the speeches of the colony's great orators—Parkes, Dibbs, Reid, Barton and a few other celebrated entertainers—but in a half inch here, an inch there, there are fidgety glimpses of W. M. Hughes, the Solidarity Labor Party Candidate in Lang. With a big sign, VOTE FOR W.M. HUGHES behind him, he speaks from hotel balconies at the Star Hotel, the Oxford Hotel, the Grace Darling Hotel. There are street corner rallies. He speaks in the Old Masonic Hall. Attendances are good... 500... 800... Addressing the 'workers and storekeepers of NSW' he speaks of the need for new blood in the lower house, the need to abolish the upper house, the need for more matters to be settled directly by the people in referendums, the need to replace the private banks with a state bank, the need to grip monopoly by the windpipe, the need to 'sink the fiscal issue' and to see the real issue as that of the Solidarity Labor Party against 'the Fat Man Party', the party of the rich...and the need to understand that *if the wealth of land and capital is to be left in the hands of the few the masses will never secure a decent livelihood*. One of Fitzgerald's meetings is broken up by Hughes supporters who shout Fitzgerald down with cries of 'Leg Irons!' and other reminders of police suppression of strikers; a minor candidate, a deserter from the Solidarity Labor Party, is pelted with stale eggs and bags of flour. But Hughes gets a good hearing. People admire the skill of his speeches; they chuckle at his caustic irony, they cheer when he ridicules the pillars of the old order. *New Order* says that *Alexander on Buchephalus was a Falstaff compared to*

Hughes on his charger with the Labor hosts behind him. Hughes was a man who would not sell us to the enemy or turn traitor.

In its last issues before the election, *New Order* appeals to *the storekeepers, farmers and wage workers of sunny New South Wales to free themselves from the fetters of the tyrants, for the first time, becoming masters of their own destiny.*

On the Saturday night before the election (it was Hughes's idea) the Solidarity Labor Party put on a monster procession. Streams from the city and suburban leagues marched to the Queen's Statue, then assembled themselves into a line half a mile long. Behind the thirty-five players of the Enterprise Brass Band and a banner saying:

> WORKERS, ARISE, AWAKE!
> OR EVER BE FALLEN!

at 8.30 they gave three cheers for Labor and marched off, with three other brass bands, illuminated drays, coloured lights, union banners and banners proclaiming the names of all the Labor candidates and people handing out 100,000 dodgers (which Hughes helped draft) giving ten good reasons why all good citizens should vote Solidarity Labor. Saturday night was the city's greatest shopping and entertainment night, in which the people paraded the streets and, by showing themselves and looking at each other, affirmed who they were and what they wanted to be. It took the procession three hours to get to Prince Alfred Park, having wound around in a route that touched on all of the electoral divisions; sometimes the spectators were so thick that they crowded from the footpath on to the street. In the procession they sang songs about their coming victory, fired off many salvoes of cheers for themselves and of groans for the newspaper proprietors. In Prince Alfred Park, in a 'Monster Meeting' beginning at half an hour before midnight, orators forecast that *the great silent vote in the city would strike the death knell of monopoly:*

when the election was over there would be a united Labor party in parliament fifty or sixty strong.

For a while, in Lang, on election day, it looked as if this might be so. The voting was finished at five o'clock. At six o'clock Hughes's supporters, who had waited outside the polling booth while the votes were counted, saw the result posted up. Their man was in! He had won by 105 votes from Taylor, the Freetrade candidate. A straight victory for Solidarity Labor! 'Opposed to me I had all the power of money,' said Hughes. 'We will go on fighting until there is a Labor government.' His supporters cheered and cheered his grand win, and drew their hero through the city in a dog cart. But in the many places where the results from the other divisions were being posted up, while there were many cheers, not many of them were for Labor. The enthusiasm had been great, the expectations had been high, but only 27 out of 125 members of parliament professed to be Labor, and of those 12 were 'Bogus'; only 15 were 'Solidarity'. The Labor Party had had the first of what were to be its many electoral disappointments.

Chapter 2

W. M. Hughes, Labor Leader

❧ The central part of Parliament House in Sydney had been built in the 1820s, as part of the general hospital put up on a ridge by Governor Macquarie in one of his first attempts to give some pretence of reason to the mess he had found all around him. It was built as the principal surgeon's residence. With its wide tropical verandahs and white columns, it still maintains some of the confident air of colonial command.

The hospital was too large, and when people who had made fortunes in the colony began demanding institutions similar to those that in the mother-country gave oligarchic freedom to British gentlemen, space—first for the supreme court, and then an executive council and a legislative council—was found in some of the unused rooms of the hospital. When a certain amount of electoral representation was allowed in 1842, a handsome new chamber was put on to one end of the former principal surgeon's residence. This was the chamber that the squatters and their offsiders were to dominate for a decade. It was here, in radical mood, that they bullied governors into legalising privileges they had already grabbed. It was here also that in the late 1840s they began preparing for self-government under a restricted voting system that would allow them and their gentlemanly city associates to run the place.

They had bad luck. Throughout the European nations there was talk of democratising old institutions by giving votes to some of 'the people'. The Australian colonies were among the first places to do this. In a mood set by 'great protest meetings' and torchlight processions, the flag of the Southern Cross, raised first in the Anti-Transportation Leagues ('We will not be slaves') and then in the uprising at Eureka ('We swear by the Southern Cross to stand by each other and fight to defend our rights and liberties'), new kinds of political leaders appeared—city merchants, lawyers, publicans, journalists, traders—who were backed by shopkeepers, skilled tradesmen, and otters seeking new dignity.

Dismissed as 'the wealthy lower orders' by the established snobs of the gentlemen's clubs and government house sets, these new men, adding to their ranks some of the shopkeepers and skilled tradesmen, took over most of the running of the elected legislative assembly which in 1856 had moved into the handsome new chamber put up in 1842 for the legislative council. Using the language of improvement and political reform, they spoke in the name of 'the people'. At the southern end of the former surgeon's residence a prefab hall bought in Melbourne was put up for the upper house, to which 'the great interests' of the colony had now retreated and from which they regularly vetoed bills sent to them from the other end of the building, claiming legitimacy from their own fundamental economic importance and traditional soundness.

Being British (an overwhelming proportion of the new members of parliament were born in the British Isles) it had not occurred to them to do anything more than ape their origins. The two 'houses' improvised at each end of the former principal surgeon's residence were seen as similar to the house of lords and the house of commons, and as necessary. The governor, in his gothic manor house with tudor extensions, seemed as irreplaceable as a monarch.

By the time Will Hughes had been elected to the seat of Lang, much of this was being challenged. The drunkenness and crookedness of many members of parliament was derided, although the voters could also show both compassion and pride towards some of parliament's greatest rogues. Some now said the upper house should go and the vote be extended. Some derided the governors. Beyond that, there was a dissatisfaction with the whole spirit of the place. Reminiscing later, Hughes spoke of it as a time when *the old order was about to pass into the new*—by which (apart from his own election to parliament) he meant a modernisation of New South Wales, with some of the more flagrant rackets of power abandoned to accommodate new forces for change. He said the *end of an epoch was at hand. The time was rotten ripe for radical reforms. The country was in the hands of a narrow-minded, purse-proud oligarchy, who controlled a legislature which made laws to serve their interest, the government that administered them, the magistracy that interpreted them, and the police that enforced them. The press, boasting of its freedom, could always be relied on to champion their cause, and to cover their reactionary and intolerant policy with rounded periods designed to delude the people into believing it to be progressive and enlightened. Constituencies had been cunningly jerrymandered to ensure the election of their chosen candidates, and the franchise gave some men four votes and many men no votes at all. But the people were determined to put an end to this state of affairs.*

On 7 August 1894, Will Hughes caught the tram from Annandale, where he was now living, into town. He was due at parliament house at noon to take his seat in the legislative assembly of New South Wales. While the couple of thousand people standing outside dwindled to a few hundred, the members took an hour and a half to be sworn in. When what turned out to be an unceremonial ceremony was over, Hughes and the other fourteen members of Solidarity Labor refused to talk to the press and met in a room where they locked the doors and discussed who their leader was to be, and how they were to behave. To the believers, they were necessary agents of great political change. *They might be few now, but they would prove a vanguard, and soon, when they were many, their time would come.*

They were to become many, but some of the great political changes were not to come. The Labor Parties were to move into parliament houses, and later to form governments, but later, and at a time when such things were becoming unthinkable in other 'parliamentary democracies', Labor governments in Australia would still be crippled by upper houses, and even dismissed by governors. What the Labor Parties were undoubtedly to achieve was to make parliaments seem more credible to those who might otherwise have doubted them. By being co-operative, the Labor Parties were to give greater legitimacy to the very institutions that would sometimes destroy them. In Hughes, taking the tram into town on 7 August, we can see the very beginnings of that process.

Imagine him and the fourteen other 'Solidarities' in their opening weeks. Hughes is not alone among them in having had only one shirt on his back, nor is he alone in enjoying for the first time in his life, an income of £300 a year. Parliament house is an excellent club; he hopes to read his way through many of the books in its library, but he can also enjoy sitting in its leather chairs, playing on its billiards tables, eating in its dining rooms. His railway pass will take him free to anywhere he wants to go in the colony; now they can't refuse him accommodation at country hotels, or kick him out of shearing sheds.

But, lest he is tempted, there are still the voices outside of those who put him there. *New Order* warns him of the hollowness of all this when it describes how *the first session of the twenty-eighth capitalistic parliament was opened with all the old world tomfoolery that still surrounds the modern statute factory, with the governor in his gold-braided clothes, with knee breeches, silk stockings, cocked hat and dyed chicken feathers and gaily dressed ladies elbowing tinsel-spangled flunkeys to get a glimpse of the show while the police keep back the crowd of ragged and hungry people.* It sees the Solidarity Party as a small band of invaders in an enemy country: *Every weapon known in the inexhaustible arsenal of political warfare would be remorselessly used to destroy them.*

But against these words—the kind of words Hughes had used from hotel balconies and street corners—must be set the realities of what is happening in parliament house. Here amongst the cigar smoke and the bustle in the corridors and public rooms he presses against the living flesh of those Mr Fats whom his supporters see as their deadliest enemies. Here they are, humans like any other. Even worse, over there is Joseph Cook leader of 'the old Labor Party' (as Cook described it) or 'the bogus Labor Party' (as Hughes described it), a Lithgow coal miner three years ago and now already sold out and become a government minister on £1500 a year, wearing a wrinkled shiny black-cloth coat with long tails, and 'moving about in a half apologetic way, as if he were a spaniel let off the chain and for the first time admitted on sufferance into a sitting room'. All around are those who have been denounced in abstract terms from spruiking boxes but now they must be greeted and dealt with as people of flesh and blood. Parliamentary radicals who have supported some Labor measures may be standoffish to the new members from the labouring classes while mad reactionaries who would clap Labor men into leg-irons may prove good drinkers or amusing storytellers. *New Order* warns that *new members could not be too careful in bastioning themselves against the wily, subverting assaults of the old parliamentary foxes.*

Imagine Hughes making his first speech in parliament. It is 29 August and he is supporting a motion that the house meet at 2 p.m. not at the 4 p.m. that suits the lawyers and stock jobbers who prefer to drop into parliament after making their money for the day. Imagine him, left hand on hip, right hand pointed, finger about to jab in the air. It is the greatest of all the initiation stages in his life—his first speech in parliament. He has caught the speaker's eye...the mouth opens...it will go on opening in parliaments for the next fifty-eight years. As a student of debating societies he is careful to offer the house some learned allusions—someone is referred to as *Curtius-like,* someone else is compared with *the renowned tailors of Tooley Street*—but the whole point of his speech is not to meet middle-class standards, but to give the debate a working-class emphasis. He attacks those who see parliament as *a refuge for gentlemen who want to get rich and bolster their privileges, heaping up wealth sometimes by rather devious and reprehensible methods,* and then, in effect, he curses them: he invokes the power of the toilers. *In their extremity,* he says, referring to recent incidents, *the toilers might burn steamboats, break down huts, kill other men's sheep*...The Speaker calls him to order. No more of that!...For a while Hughes is a debating society orator again. Then he lashes out a second time...The Speaker again calls him to order...He obeys, plays straight, then again hits out...He is again called to order, and warned. The next day the *Daily Telegraph* attacks his speech; at the end of the week *New Order* boasts that, in his currycombing of the lawyers, he was gagged three times. Hughes has appealed to the audience he wants to please; he has shown he is loyal to his class.

Between then and Christmas he speaks twenty-eight times, sometimes simply, in short interventions, sometimes in set pieces. He flourishes occasional allusions, with references to Gyges' Ring, Columbus, Macaulay, Elizabeth and Mary, Mrs Partington with her broom, *hoi polloi,* but right through till Christmas his basic mode is to speak the emotional language of class. Some of the rest of what he says may be humdrum... the right of ordinary people to buy pastry and a bottle of ginger beer on a Sunday, the need of fruit-growers for half-price ammunition so that they can shoot flying foxes, the need for a better water supply on the Wyalong goldfield, the price of horse feed in the country... but he regularly shows that his heart is in the right place, and when he does speak significantly, it is on safe labour movement issues... payment of members, the land tax, strikebreaking.

If this class rhetoric is removed from everything else he says and considered in itself, Hughes can be made seem a revolutionary, concerned only with *the wretchedness, misery and degradation that came from the bolstering of private monopoly in an accursed system which now meant that within a stone's throw from the parliament building men were herding together like pigs. As machinery was becoming more and more perfected, the working classes were becoming extinct; the labourer had become an automaton who did not know anything except that he caught hold of a lever and pulled it. The small storekeeper and struggling tradesmen who had always voted for the law and order crowd had been crushed out of existence by the syndicates, as if they had been swept under the wheels of the car of Juggernaut. Now the very rich and the very poor were standing out and there was a yawning gulf between them with no middle class to span it over. And beneath the profession of law and order, the violence of the state provoked rebellion and bloodshed. If the monopolists' interests were threatened by a strike, the whole available police force would be sent, in a sinful incitement to rebellion, to a peaceful and law abiding population. And while the army of the unemployed grew, the militarists built up a totally unnecessary army in a country that was 10,000 miles away from danger. The ominous warnings of military threat were simply bogies intended to justify a standing army. But where would such an invasion come from?*

Then in a solemn manner, especially if he is interrupted, he will bring down a fearsome curse. He will throw against his opponents the threat of the people's vengeance: *If the government didn't deal with the unemployment crisis the people would deal with them and when it dealt with them there would be nothing left of the government. Make no mistake. This was the last and desperate attempt of the people, and if their lot was not ameliorated, the exploiters would be simply obliterated.*

Someone laughs...Hughes turns and lays a curse on him:

he reminds him that when strikers were attacked in the United States they defended themselves with Winchester rifles.

Yet Hughes is not advocating revolution. In one speech he won't even use the word. He refers instead, euphemistically, to *an alteration* and *an alteration so speedy*. In another speech he says the problem is to find employment for men who are hungry, *ill-clothed and wretched. This is not revolution. It is the essence of conservatism. It is to conserve society*. He has two answers to what must be done—large estates and land monopoly must be broken up, along with the even more powerful industrial monopolies of the capitalist system. But when it comes to dealing with existing unemployment, although he has previously been at his most sarcastic in telling members how ignorant they are of economics—wondering whether 'claptrap' or 'balderdash' is the better word to describe them—the best he can suggest is putting men on to piece work, clearing and fencing 40,000 or 50,000 acres (16,000 to 20,000 hectares) of land, then, by letting it to suitable tenants, establishing village settlements, taking reasonable care that *the communistic spirit is not carried too far*. What he wants is the growth of *a class of yeomanry—the most desirable class of men in any country*.

From these first four months of what was to end up being Hughes's 687 months in parliament one can see in miniature not only the shape of his own future political problems, but part of the whole troubled future of the Labor Party. With his belief in the destruction of capitalistic monopoly and his professed socialism, Hughes was declaredly on the left wing of a party officially committed only to a land tax, a state bank, the problems of the small prospector-miner and a compulsory eight-hour day; of the fifteen 'Solidarities' only Hughes and another four were declared socialists, but the kind of rhetoric he used was common throughout the movement. How much he and the others believed this rhetoric, we cannot say. Was extra sharpness given to the socialism of Hughes, Holman, the

New Order group, the central executive committee and other supporters of Solidarity Labor in 1894 because they were battling to destroy 'the old Labor Party' by proclaiming it 'bogus' and taking its members' seats? One never knows where belief ends and self interest begins; all one can do is listen to what politicians say, and then look at what they do. What Hughes and others were saying was that destruction of land monopolies and capitalist industrial monopolies was essential to human betterment. What they were doing was using their strength in parliament, such as it was, to support a freetrade government with a minor reform program which included imposing income and land taxes, and bringing in some changes for small farmers, some improvements in working conditions in ships, factories and mines and a system of local government. So here was one of the first working-class parties in the world to sit in a bourgeois parliament and some of its members were saying one thing (speaking in the voice of socialism) but doing another (politely participating in the rituals of parliament and discussing the price of horse feed or the availability of ginger beer on Sundays). They drew rhetoric from the disasters of unemployment and the distress of the terrible economic depression that was testing the colony; they might even conjure out of unemployment apocalyptic visions of revolution; but since they believed that reform was not possible without the abolition of land monopoly and capitalism, they could not offer any remedying reform for the troubled times.

Leave Hughes there in parliament for a moment, frozen in some characteristic gesture, perhaps thundering against the violence the worker suffers from the state, perhaps thundering against the flying foxes attacking the fruit trees, and look ahead to what is going to happen to the Labor Party over the next six years...

For the next six years the Solidarity Labor Party remains minor, with only 19 out of 125 members by the end of the decade, and until 1898 not even holding the balance of power. To many outsiders it seems on its way out, or, at best, a small pressure group representing a minority interest. To many of its own supporters it is the natural majority party: they calculate their potential support on a base of economic class and argue that since 80% of voters are wage earners, Labor should swamp parliament by gaining 80% of the vote. When this fails to happen they blame the unfairness and antagonism of the capitalist press, arguing that newspapers present a conveniently false reality by 'fooling and diverting the wage earners with false issues'.

They try to provide organisational strength in the party's branches and the trades unions, but this doesn't work. Many party branches scarcely exist, except for the exciting sport of election time, and some unions remain so weakened that they are barely alive. In the manner of politics, union leaders active in the party sometimes intervene, mainly to express jealousies and suspicions of each other, or of their brothers who sit in parliament on £300 a year. By the end of the decade Labor is not even established as the main party of reform. It is not Labor but the major parties that throw up the great issues of poor against rich and of democracy against privilege; for another decade the language of progress and reform remains the general language of politics—by standards prevailing in the European nations New South Wales seems a 'social laboratory', a vanguard of social change. The Labor Party can sometimes seem a minor party running after the bandwagon.

In the union press, headlines, cartoons and verse continue to depict a simple world of class warfare, with on one side the toilers, tall, lean, forthright, upholding freedom and justice and, on the other side 'Mr Fat', the bloated capitalist in his top hat, with as henchman the crooked politicians, the bought press, the corrupt judges and the lackeys of government house. The Labor MPs both speak this language and don't speak it. They speak it because they believe it, or because it is what gets a good cheer at meetings, or because without using it they will lose their pre-selections; they don't speak it because on many occasions, if they get down to particular details, it is irrelevant, or if they appeal to special interests, this language may offend some of them.

Their agonies of choice come from the dilemma that while machines and the new factory civilisation have thrown up a new class, the wage earners, and many of them take collective pride in seeing themselves as 'workers', it has also thrown up other kinds of wage earners, usually working in shops and offices and government agencies, who see themselves not as 'workers' but as 'employees' with 'careers'. To the worker, honour comes from being a worker. So long as a worker remains loyal to the working class no one can take such honour away. To the employee, honour has to be earned, by obtaining advancement through diligence. Even many manual workers do not see themselves as 'workers'. Economic changes that created the working class have also created the suburbs that can weaken the consciousness of there being a working class. A visiting Englishman writes of the 'petty suburban proprietor' who sits on his verandah on sunny Sunday mornings, smoking, and airing his views with fellow workmen. A visiting Frenchman writes: 'if the forward march, for the working class, consists of attaining the exact level of the bourgeoisie, the manual worker of Australia has raised himself as high as possible'.

It is to this background, between 1895 and 1898 that Hughes stops speaking of himself as a 'socialist'. In the 1895 elections, seven of the eighteen successful Labor candidates are socialists, including Hughes; and in 1896 at the annual Labor conference Hughes is part of a socialist majority which uses its numbers to add to the platform a plank calling for the nationalisation of all coal, silver, copper and iron mines and the establishment of state mills and depots for sugar, grain and produce, and of state farms and labour colonies to absorb the unemployed. The next year a militant socialist majority nails socialism itself to the mast, with a declaration written into the platform that the party believes in nationalising land and the whole means of production, distribution and exchange. But by then Hughes is a moderate, intolerant of such militancy, and he and Holman and their Leigh House friends, along with the Australian Workers' Union, stack the next conference so that the idea of state mills, depots, farms and mines goes out of the platform and nationalisation is reduced to the second last plank in a platform of twenty-five. For the rest of Hughes's time in the Labor Party a general nationalisation is off the agenda. Hughes resigns from the Australian Socialist League when it breaks off in 1898 to form its own Socialist Labor Party. The Political Labor League (as the Labor Party renames itself) is dismissed by former associates as 'a mere vote-catching machine' and Hughes is denounced as 'Hughes, the one time socialist'.

By then the Labor Party, with Hughes in the van, is fighting its way into another defeat. The Party is to struggle unsuccessfully to stop the colonies federating on the basis of a constitution seen as so undemocratic by Labor that it is explained as a capitalist and conservative reaction to the rising wave of democracy. For two and a half years, in three campaigns, Hughes fights against the proposed constitution. In the manner of a campaigner, he switches and swivels, but constantly he attacks a document which because it will be so hard to amend, he describes as *a mousetrap—once in, never get out,* and a senate which he sees as *an upper house, not to conserve state rights but to retard social reform.* He urges the citizens of New South Wales not to impose an American constitution on a British system but to look for an Australian constitution, meeting Australian needs, and at his most inflamed he warns against *a constitution which is already darkened by the shadow of carnage and deadly strife, and which invites disaster and revolution.* In the last lonely campaign, in a desperate measure, instead of concluding campaign meetings with the customary three cheers for Australia, he calls for three cheers for democracy.

Then, in the manner of a politician, once it is all over and he has taken his beating, he comes up wagging his tail. When he is put on to a committee to plan the federation procession in Sydney on New Year's Day, 1901, the day an English earl will proclaim the new Commonwealth, Hughes throws himself into this with such vigour that he even helps with preparing some of the horses. When the great day dawns, Hughes's contribution is this: as part of the ten-kilometre long procession, with its detachments of Life Guards, Hussars, Sikhs, Gurkhars, and colonial troops and its carriages containing the Mr Fats, there is a trades union section, with bushworkers riding on horses behind a group of shearers, the eight-hour day banner held aloft behind the railway band and a group of other unionists in working costume carrying their tools of trade. It is remarkable that trade unionists should be seen in such a procession: it would not happen in the capitals of Europe. But was it remarkable as a symbol of the unions' strength or of the compliance of the unions, and their desire to seek the earl's respect?

Now return to Hughes, in 1894, a new member yet to make his way, frozen in a characteristic gesture. Imagine he finishes his gesture, and his speech, leaves the debating chamber, and starts telling yet another anecdote: perhaps it is the anecdote of how he got his Labor pre-selection. It goes on for ages...he wanted a constituency within the radius of a penny tram section from parliament...when he picked Lang a rival candidate closed the books of the branch to stop Hughes supporters from enrolling...on the first night the ballot lasted till midnight...there were two more ballots on successive nights, finally with only Hughes and one other candidate...at the last ballot, in a packed hall, he chose as scrutineers his two largest supporters, both carrying wool hooks... those voting for him scrounged other people's electors' rights so that they could vote often as well as early... the chairman announced in thunderous tones that the ballot was closed. The narrow street was crowded; an air of suppressed excitement prevailed;

Hughes waited near the door trying to look like a man supremely confident of victory; words dropped out of his mouth mechanically as he waited for the verdict, straining his ears for the first murmurs that meant the numbers were up. Suddenly, the end comes. The crowd, which had been unnaturally quiet, springs to life. A roar bursts upon his ears. 'What is it?' he asks. 'You've been selected', says a friend. 'Run for your life!'

In his first six years in the legislative assembly Hughes learned to become a 'parliamentarian'. He learned the rules so well that they became instinctive, like tricks learned in law courts. They could be used in a permanent game of adversary advantage, in which contest becomes an aristocratic tournament conducted for its own sake. He was clever at taking points of order, asking embarrassing questions, parrying dangerous interjections, exaggerating useful differences, stretching out an opponent's argument until it snapped from its own absurdity. With three political parties in the ring, and all three, within that decade, disloyal around the edges, he could also see parliament as a place for disappointed men to switch sides, try to wreck their old allies, and perhaps succeed—and still survive. And, like a true parliamentarian, he could become enormously absorbed in the trivia of life in parliament— who scored this point or that, who spoke best, what they were gossiping about in the corridors—as if all the power and all the conflict in society was contained inside the walls of parliament house.

This was the time when Hughes was becoming 'little Willie'. In his constituency a few blocks down King Street, he could also be spoken of, in a sense of awed affection, as 'the little man', or 'little Hughes', or, sometimes, 'Billy' (a diminutive he detested). As 'little Willie' he was seen as remorseless, with biting invective, fierce sarcasm, clever verbal parries, cutting, slashing, convincing, appealing to the head not the heart. But despite all the fierceness that came from his mouth and his gestures, people could love him from a distance for his gameness, his smallness, his humour, even his trickiness, and his ability to appear always as nothing grander than a fellow creature, as if all men really were brothers.

In the theatre of parliamentary 'debate', so important to Hughes, by the time he left the New South Wales parliament he was one of its most celebrated and enjoyable performers—if the word went around that 'little Hughes was up' members were likely to return to the debating chamber. He was also capable of daring impromptus, even in the debating chamber, giving reality and concreteness to an argument by making up an anecdote. Attacking what he sees as the waste of money in supporting armies in the Australian colonies when there is no military threat against them, to strengthen a point he suddenly invents a tale about how he enrolled in the Queensland army during a Russian war scare of 'ten or twelve years ago' (when he was still in London). Yet he had not forgotten that power also lay outside parliament. His constituency was becoming one of the most reliably Labor in the world; the people who lived there were aware of the past disasters of weakness and saw the need to come to the aid of the party. Hughes and the faithful coal lumper who was chairman of his branch and his other waterfront allies were determined that he would not fight another ballot for pre-selection. Throughout the annual meetings, the money-raising socials, the dances and fetes, the debating nights and the speech nights, the canvasses of voters to enrol and the drives for party membership at four shillings a head, VOTE W. M. HUGHES remained one of the self-evident triumphs of Darling Habour.

Hughes's repertoire of anecdotes expands until it becomes the man and Hughes acts like a character in a Will Hughes story. Life has become Dickensian, a matter of caricature, its absurdities made bearable by a simplifying jocularity. A characteristic story will be the story of how he and another Labor member, on a country tour organising branches, make themselves seem more important than they are, by passing themselves off as a select committee of parliament, recommending sites for new railway stations. They receive deputations, make promises; at one town they are greeted by a civic welcome and a brass band playing *See the Conquering Hero Comes*.

He begins to act as if people are nothing more than cardboard cut-outs assembled in the play corner. Or, to put it more exactly and more compassionately, whatever feeling for the sadness of things there may be in his heart, he acts outwardly as if people are figurines, to be moved here and there to simplify a tale. Since politics makes caricatures of us all, this Dickensian imagination is to be of some advantage to him as a politician; but it will mean that when he appeals to ordinary supporters he can lack ordinary feeling—unless there is a maudlin Dickensian sense of melodrama to appeal to. He finds satisfying melodrama, however, in the plight of the workers; then his talent for melodrama will reach full flood in the hate and tears of the Great War.

At the end of the decade W. M. Hughes was to build himself his own trades union. Unions had disintegrated on the waterfront after the collapse of the 1890 strike, and for the rest of the decade the stevedoring and shipping companies could do what they liked. With no effective unions and with so many unemployed, they kept wages low and hired and fired as they chose. If men tried to form new unions the owners would blacklist those who joined and hunt their organisers off the wharves. In this blackened, empty and threatened landscape Hughes moved silently and cunningly: for three months at the end of 1899 he assembled a group of organisers who secretly enrolled 1,300 members into a Wharf Labourers' Union. On 27 December with this secret background of solid organisation, he called a meeting of the new union and had himself elected secretary. Two days later, the whole operation now retrospectively legitimised, he called another meeting, a grand affair, in which the union was given an impelling 1880s style respectability—on the platform were the premier, the minister for works, ten MPs, an Anglican archdeacon and the Catholic parish priest. By this and other bluffs, and by not risking any confrontation that the union could lose, Hughes was able to nurse weaknesses and, to both owners and workers, give the union an appearance of strength.

In this he was a fox. In declaring and maintaining his own personal dominance of the union, he was a lion. 'A breaker down of obstacles and a leader of men', he would face up to a meeting of wharfies, and plead, ridicule and bully them into seeing it his way; individual opponents would be hunted into a corner, and killed with the collective strength he had summoned.

When he claimed a safe Labor constituency (based on the Sydney waterfront) in the federal parliament that was to meet in Melbourne in May 1901 (its proceedings to be opened by an English prince dressed as a British admiral) he had gained one of the few safe Labor seats in Australia. And now that the Sydney waterfront was organised behind him both politically and industrially he could also imagine another kind of power: he had tasted a middle-class success. As a successful crusader for the Early Closing Association, with speeches and political pressuring, he helped bring about the great social reform of reducing the working week in the shops from its early Dickensian proportions, and enjoyed the new pleasure of gaining the support of people who saw themselves as anti-Labor. Through this he also gained the esteem of the middle-class leaders of the early closing movement. They gave him a gold watch.

He was reading for law. He had moved house a couple of times to better class suburbs, and now he would cross the harbour, and live on the North Shore, a ferry ride away from the waterfront where his main power still lay. But with all this success there was disaster. His wife, who had helped him with his shop, and who had by now borne seven children (one of whom had died), had not been able to stay by the side of such a fast mover. She did not meet the new kinds of people he knew. He did not pass on to her his new kinds of ideas. As he conquered new worlds, she was left at home, puzzled, resentful, and now in ill health.

As Hughes ran his union and his constituency and read his law books and played the games of parliament and campaigned as a public figure and quarrelled with his wife in a disorganised household with six children, he was driven on not only by ambition but by the hard, bleak force of his own stubborn cantankerousness.

***

Since they connected the two main cities in Australia, the Melbourne Express and the Sydney Express made up Australia's most prestigious and fashionable train service. Their first-class carriages, whether at Melbourne Cup time, or the opening of a new parliament, or indeed on any night of the week, were likely to bring together the rich, the powerful, the influential and the celebrated. They were a 'club' where rulers of all kinds (of high society, or business, or politics, or the professions) might meet in a way not possible in the Melbourne Club or the Union Club (where some of them would have been blackballed). Rich and powerful and famous people would visit friends in their compartments; or stand in the corridor, gaining prestige by trading gossip and perhaps helping to form some new general opinion.

Towards the end of May 1909, imagine a compartment in which sit the attorney general of Australia, and a ministerial messenger. The messenger, acting as private secretary, is working at a typewriter on the table. The minister is curled up in a corner, fountain pen in hand, scribbling out notes for a speech. W. M. Hughes has been attorney general for six months in a Labor government thrown up in one of the moves in parliament's game of musical chairs, but government hasn't yet meant much to him; most of it has been spent in recess, handling routine matters. However, Andrew Fisher the Prime Minister (an Ayrshire miner so Scottish that at times native Australians can't understand what he is talking about) has announced a program in a 34,000 word address to his electors in a Queensland mining town and Hughes is now travelling down to Melbourne to hear the governor-general read out a summary of this program in his official opening of the parliamentary session in the Victorian parliament house, borrowed until the national capital is built.

Hughes is now forty-six and this improvised life has become his style. Earlier, when he was reading for the Bar (he became a barrister in 1903) he would study his law books on the Melbourne Express. For a while he would take a portable phonograph to play records of great orators. And in the Melbourne Express he conducts union business, political business, constituency business, and scribbles out speeches and articles.

His wife emerged from her sickliness and died nearly three years ago, leaving him a sad letter written only two weeks before she died: 'Good night, Will: always remember this: that once I loved you very dearly and tho we may drift apart in the future I shall always remain, Your Faithful Wife E. Hughes'. In Melbourne he has lived in boarding houses (for a while most of the Labor members lived in the one boarding house) or rented accommodation (he was unsuccessfully sued for damage to furniture in a house rented for three months in 1904). When his wife died he made his eighteen-year-old daughter Ethel his housekeeper, and gave her the job of bringing up the four younger children, with some help from her elder brother. Now he is contemplating sending them to private schools in Melbourne, the boys to Melbourne Grammar, the girl to the Methodist Ladies' College.

W. M. Hughes sees himself as the brains of the Labor Party and is ready to share his vision with anyone who will listen. For this reason he is a man of disappointed ambition in a party that, he feels, can be prejudiced against brilliance. He feels he may never get quite to the top. When the deputy leadership went up for the vote in 1905, it was Andrew Fisher, not Hughes, who won it, and Fisher is the same age as Hughes. Now Fisher is prime minister. Although Hughes is second on the cabinet list and outside parliament may be the most widely known of the Labor members, inside the party they see him differently: he is not 'a good caucus man'; sometimes he doesn't even turn up at caucus meetings; he has only one close associate in the parliamentary party.

He is as busy as an ant. After forming the Sydney Wharf Labourers' Union, he organised the Trolley, Draymen and Carters' Union for the men who brought the goods from the wharves to the warehouses, becoming its president while remaining secretary of the Wharf Labourers' Union; when the State Arbitration Court was founded he did much of the work in gaining awards for both unions (minimum rates, an eight hour day, preference for unionists). He was also the main organiser of the national Waterside Workers' Union, that gathered men from ports all around the Australian coast under a leadership consisting mainly of Labor MPs; when this was established he became its president. There are other men to do the day-to-day work in these unions, but as much as he can, Hughes keeps in touch with even the routine work—whenever he is in Sydney he attends weekly meetings—and he still holds power to initiate all general policy and negotiation. Even when he is attorney-general, he is still running his unions.

As a barrister, he does a lot of business not only for the unions he has organised, but for a number of other waterfront unions. He gets briefs in straightforward union cases that get into the arbitration courts and also the appeals to superior courts that often follow them. Other unions hire him as a legal advisor or negotiator and from the briefs in workers' compensation cases for individual union members he gains the kind of income which enables him to send his children to private schools. When he publishes his book *The Case for Labor* the by-line says *By W. M. Hughes, M.H.R., (Barrister-at-Law)*.

It is as a union magnate and trouble fixer that W. M. Hughes gets the most publicity. There are times when, in the newspapers, he can seem the central figure of the day, a man who always wins—and can even win praise from the newspapers. (In one strike the *Sydney Morning Herald* tells 'the more demonstrative' waterfront workers to listen 'to that reason which a man of Mr Hughes' experience and education' can offer.) In the months-long waterfront disputes in 1908 Hughes seems to play a large part of the cast of characters—as Sydney Wharf Labourers' Union secretary he negotiates with himself as Waterside Workers' Federation president to avoid a general strike in Newcastle; he seeks his support as president of the Trolley, Draymen and Carters' Union to help the strikers in Sydney; he puts in a good word for the strikers with himself as legal adviser to the Merchant Service Guild. In the newspapers he seems everywhere: he is at a meeting at the trades hall...then, a dapper figure, skipping the puddles as nimbly as a Persian cat, nodding to acquaintances here and there like a debutante at a garden party, he is off to a mass meeting of 3,400 men on a wharf...tile iron gates of the wharf shut...sounds of applause come to the reporters standing outside in the rain...with the meeting over, W. M. Hughes holds a press conference sitting on a sack of potatoes...He confers with the premier, the joint executive of the unions, the shipowners: at night he gives a press conference in his North Shore house. As it turns out, he out-tricks the owners and, hands down, wins the strike. On other occasions he wins by preventing strikes. The readers of newspapers are becoming accustomed to the idea of W. M. Hughes as a man who appears when there is trouble, who goes through great travail, then emerges with victory.

For amusing himself with something else at the weekends, he buys a 75-acre dairy farm on the river flats at Wilberforce, a Macquarie town on the Hawkesbury, where he puts in a member of the Carters' Union to run it as a share farmer. At first he relaxes with nothing more energetic to do than tell 'little Hughes' stories. But he can't keep still; he wants to weed out the herd, then double, then treble the number of milkers; obsessed by visions of fat cheques, he consults the experts; they tell him he must grow his own lucerne, and for that he needs irrigation plant; he buys a second-hand engine and pumping plant. Now he can relax by spending the weekend working.

Then all this turns into a 'little Hughes' story—of discord and crazy battle. The new man he puts in tries to blackmail him for illegal use of official postage stamps; Hughes sacks him, but the man claims to be a share farmer partner and refuses to go; Hughes comes back with a small commando of neighbours and men from the Carters' Union, holding iron bars, clubs and other improvised weapons. They fight it out against five defenders who use a gymnasium club, an axe handle and lengths of wood. Hughes's head is broken, but, on the third assault, the defenders are thrown out. Their furniture is thrown out after them. When the case comes up in court, Hughes loses and pays £150 for assault and £100 for breach of contract. The allegations about illegal use of stamps are finally silenced several years later by one of the boys from the trades hall.

The story has so much of the future in it that it might be seen as a morality play, forecasting madness to come. Of the future, it foretells all the busyness, the running around, the allegations of crookedness and deceit and the playground excitements of improvised conflict. In the comic foray against the farmhouse by the Nyms and Bardolphs and Pistols of the Carters' Union, led by a Falstaff as skinny as a radish, and growing bold on stomach powders rather than on sack, there are, in comedy, shadowy intimations of what will soon be told in tragedy—those thousands of assaults on farmhouses that in a few years will help make the French countryside an ossuary.

***

Federation had proved disappointing. The deal put together by conservative politicians as the Commonwealth

Constitution (and ratified by 42.01% of the electors) had been made in such a spirit of pragmatism that one spokesman for federation gave as his justification for it: 'We shall create a glorious nation and meat will be cheaper'. The new constitution was neither an expression of any democratic aspiration, nor of national inspiration. It had not been fought for by war or revolution; unlike the constitutions the colonies themselves had gained it had not been associated even with agitation in the streets and town halls. A common view was that Australia was not a 'nation'. All that had happened was that the colonial politicians had come to a new arrangement.

This very emptiness of 'purpose' in the constitution may have given sharp, extra meaning to the idea of 'Australia for the White Man'. In Canada there was a 'White Canada' movement and there was agitation against coloured immigrants in the United States. But in neither country was race chauvinism used as the exclusive means of defining the nation, alone giving it public identity and purpose. In Australia it was given this function. This unique emphasis may have been provided by the accident that in 1901 a federation had occurred without proper rhetorical warning: federation was given retrospective meaning by the Commonwealth's implementation of the White Australia policy. Immigration restriction was not one of the prime purposes of federation, but when the newly-elected MPs met in Melbourne in their borrowed houses they had to act like statesmen, who had some important occasion for their coming together. They needed a great self-defining debate: that ritual debate proved to be on immigration policy. It was not even a debate—only two speakers raised any doubts. It was a ceremony of affirmation that the prime national purpose of Australia was to be a continent of unique racial purity.

In creating the idea of the Australian nation as the world's most racially pure society the Labor Party led all the others, and of all its supporters W. M. Hughes was one of the loudest and clearest. In election campaigning he saw Labor's chief plank as the White Australia policy. In the great debate in Melbourne he saw that *a free people on the very threshold of their national career must not only fear the destruction of living standards that would come with cheap coloured labour; these coloured people must also be rejected because of their vices, because of their immorality, and because of a hundred things which could only be hinted.*

To the creation of an idea of an Australian nation through racism Hughes has added the creation of an idea of an Australian nation through a democratic army. As we imagine W. M. Hughes scribbling with his fountain pen in a corner of his compartment in the Melbourne Express while the ministerial messenger types out letters, we might also imagine that what he is writing are notes for yet another speech to the National Defence League of Australia. He is editor of their magazine, *The Call,* and, with an army colonel, their joint honorary secretary. He has gone on national speaking campaigns for them, travelling over a thousand kilometres in a week, making a speech a night. Ten years before, in his work for the Early Closing Association, he learned something of the world of middle-class reform; along with other Labor leaders, he is now a companion of professors, bishops, service officers and legislative council politicians, but some of his new associates are not middle-class reformers; they come from an upper-class world of high reaction.

The thirty-two-year-old socialist who in 1894 made fun of the idea that Australia could ever be in any danger has now become the forty-six-year-old attorney-general urging universal conscription. He has done this without shifting much of his original position. He still sees Australia as being in small danger. *Perhaps it was the least vulnerable part of the Empire. But since the British, in grabbing fresh portions of empire were sapping their strength, there was danger that if Australia tied itself wholly to a British naval power over whose policy it had no control, it might be abandoned in time of war, and open to bombardment. The most efficient way in which Australia could aid the Empire was to provide for its own defence.* Hughes is still suspicious of a military caste: *its members might be antagonistic to democratic practices and ideals; a standing army might overawe citizens in pursuit of constitutional reform or maintaining civil liberties; democracy could perish under the heel of military despotism.* The way out is to have a democratic army, a people's army, modelled on the Swiss militia, *with citizens undergoing short periods of training, but always available, so that if the call came the people would be armed, as once were the archers of England. This was not conscription: conscription produced militarism. This was universal military training, which destroyed militarism. Conscription produced a caste; universal training placed all men on one level.*

As W. M. Hughes made what was to be an annual speech in parliament on the need for self-defence forces, and gave his many speeches in mechanics institutes, schools of arts and town halls, what he was projecting was not the future—as those who chose to admire him would later assert, transforming this little man into an heroic figure foretelling the great perils of Australia, its need to arm and its need to send off gallantly loyal expeditions. He was projecting a vision that came to nothing. The idea of an independent-minded people in arms, sustained by a democratic and national spirit, self-reliant in self-defence, would have required a cultural revolution, and while a few bohemian intellectuals and probably many ordinary people might imagine such a change, none of them was a politician. All that survived from Hughes's campaigning was the idea of compulsion.

And when compulsory training of males over fourteen did come into effect, unaccompanied by any other social change, an anti-conscriptionist Australian Freedom League formed (finally with 55,000 members) and of the 40,000 boys eligible in the second year of compulsion only 17,000 registered. For over two years, defaulters were prosecuted at the rate of more than 250 per week. It was to be a militia without democracy, and a militia with no national base.

***

There is another purpose for which one might imagine W. M. Hughes as using his fountain pen in the Melbourne Express: one might imagine him scribbling out for the Sydney *Daily Telegraph* one of the series of Saturday columns that he began writing in October 1907, and would go on writing until 1911. Under the catchline *The Case for Labor* these provide the most talented and sustained attempt to throw up an ambit of belief for a party so taciturn in saying what it was supposed to be doing that its platform began with defined objectives that read like random jottings in a shopping list. In his *Daily Telegraph* columns Hughes tried to reach out to people and provide something with more human meaning.

Summarized, central parts of his rhetoric ran like this:
The capitalist world was a nightmare in which women worked for a wage shamefully inadequate to maintain them, and men risked death every day fearlessly, uncomplainingly, for a pittance so paltry that a very large number had barely the means to support themselves and their dependents for one week ahead, and some lived, literally, from hand to mouth. Even those who got regular work were merely helpless appendages; trained to do only one thing, men of one talent only, their lives were a round of deadly monotony; and to keep their jobs they were forced to order themselves lowly and submissively, or they would assuredly have had to make way for more subservient and discreet men. But many did not even get regular work; in normal seasons they worked intermittently, in bad seasons not at all. They existed and suffered in order that the employer might economically carry on his business. If it were not for them a sufficient staff would have had to have been kept on through slack seasons. To avoid this, the unemployed man was

deliberately manufactured by the smug-faced, round bellied men of private enterprise.

With an army of unfortunates chained to their ringbolts in the industrial inferno, Liberty, the equal birthright of all, of which modern society loved to prate, was for the majority a narrow and treacherous path winding round a precipitous canyon. The smug-faced, round-bellied men, upon whom the sun shone every day, said—and perhaps believed—that every man had his chance. So had every pigeon rising from the trap a chance, or thought it had— as with wildly-fluttering heart it offered up a prayer of thanksgiving and fell, choked with blood, to make a sportsman's holiday. For while socially and politically we were all free—in theory, at any rate—economically we were in chains.

In the spirit of ruthless greed now animating modern society the round-bellied men spoke of individualism, free competition, and survival of the fittest, in which one was free to get rich and one was free to stay poor, and in which the State should allow the combatants in the industrial ring to fight their own battles. But when men said that such and such was the natural law, what they generally meant was that they did not desire a chance, lest a turn of the wheel should place them in a less favorable environment, and that, if need be, the State and the Law should protect them in their present circumstances.

In any case it was no longer individualism and competition, but monopoly that dominated modern society. The day of the small employer was gone; the day of the Behemoths of Industry was upon us. The death knell of competition could no longer be denied. This was the day of the trust and the combine, that is, the regulation of production and of price for the benefit of a very few enormously wealthy persons. Yesterday trusts had been confined within the comparatively narrow limits of nations. Today they had spread their tentacles over the whole world.

But the day of the great trusts would be a small one. Their very greatness would be their undoing. It challenged the enmity of all mankind and, although their fall would be terrific, it could not be far distant. With competition already dead in many industries, and dying in others, and the question being not one of competition versus co-operation, but of co-operation for the benefit of the few versus co-operation for the benefit of the many, there could and would be but one answer. And that answer was neither more nor less than the substitution of national co-operation for the present competitive system in the industrial sphere. Under socialism the State would own and control the means of production, distribution and exchange. Private property in all other forms of wealth would remain, and other institutions, social and political, would not be affected by the change. Socialism thus involved an economic change, but not necessarily a political or social change.

This change, an inevitable consequence of modern industrialism and a necessary stage in the evolution of society, would grow and develop at its own pace and in its own way, just as manhood came to a boy. There was no such thing as voting for socialism. Socialism wanted no voting for; it only wanted room to grow and move. It would not be brought about by an act of parliament—nor by a general strike, or an armed revolt. The belief that socialism could be achieved by any coup, violent or peaceful, could only be entertained by those who failed utterly to understand not only what socialism was, but what those factors which make for change were. Socialism would replace individualism because it was fitter to survive in a new environment. Competition would be replaced by co-operation because the environment which made competition desirable had changed. And when complete collectivism arrived, to those who lived under it, it would appear the most ordinary, natural and inevitable thing in the world. Its growth would have been so gradual as to almost escape attention.

In the meantime governments would naturally continue to modify the environment in the industrial sphere, where modern methods of production had created new conditions. The State would continue with legislation such as factory and early closing acts, land tax and closer settlement acts, industrial arbitration acts and other methods of increasing economic and industrial systematisation and it would extend its own functions as an employer. In this situation those who despaired of all political action, declaring instead for a general strike or a revolution, were supporting anarchy, the very negation of socialism. And while it is true that as the combines, trusts, vends and rings stalked roughshod over the land the wage-earners had to fight bitterly and long for better conditions, nevertheless union discipline had to be more rigid: the welfare of thousands should not be imperilled by the reckless acts of a mere handful; no one union should be allowed to plunge a whole country into industrial chaos; if action was to be taken, it should be taken only after all of those affected or likely to be affected had been consulted. Now the whole effort of the Labor Party was to substitute order for chaos in the industrial and economic spheres. Until quite recently the laws had been made by the rich for their own benefit. Now all was changed; the laws were as the people made them.

As a rival show to W. M. Hughes's attempts to throw up a magic circle of belief about how human beings might become better was the brilliant art-rhetoric of Alfred Deakin, a Victorian politician who had become the stage hypnotist of the national parliaments. In the period of 'three elevens'—of Deakin's Protectionist Party, the Labor Party and the Free Trade Party—Deakin's mesmeric talent summoned up the progressive centre-position that had more or less provided a common program for the three parties as they took their turns in government. With Labor's support, he and his party had the longest spells in office, but even when they were out of office his speech-making set the agenda. In the world of Deakin's rhetoric *the machinery of state was to be employed to cope with the very great injustices which at present beset our social system, so that citizens might enjoy equal laws and opportunities, healthy lives, honest toil, fair wages, fair prices and fair conditions of employment, safeguarded by the State from cheap imported goods made by the serf labour of less happy lands and from poverty, distress, antagonism, prejudice and racial discord.* Brought together under the overall name of 'the New Protection', Deakin's promises made up one of the few attempts at a distinctively argued political theology that could seem uniquely Australian.

But, talk as quickly as he might in his long, flowing sentences, in what was seen as Australia's greatest oratory, Deakin cannot talk his way out of what now seems the collapse of the system of 'the three elevens'. His own party has split; each of the other parties outnumbers him; apart from his voice, and his eloquence, and the glow of his reputation he now has not much else behind him than the support of the Melbourne *Age*. The growth of the Labor Party has put his kind of liberalism out of business.

Now imagine that after Hughes gets out of the Melbourne Express at Spencer Street Station and goes to the attorney-general's offices, he learns that Deakin's Protectionist Party has fused with the Freetraders into a 'Liberal Party' that outnumbers Labor, with Deakin as front man, and Joseph Cook, who deserted Labor in 1894, as second in command. The Fisher government's proposals for a fine new world won't last beyond the day the governor-general reads them out in parliament. Now at the head of all his opponents since federation, and with an old supporter now in opposition crying out 'Judas', the day after the governor-general's speech, Deakin's force will be used to bring about Labor's quick execution.

***

Hughes was the first and loudest in claiming the political centre that Deakin had deserted. He set himself up in it on the very day of the execution, and from it cursed Deakin cleverly and memorably: *Every reactionary in the Commonwealth was massed behind Deakin. There was not a vested interest in the country that had not acclaimed him as their champion. The great vested interests needed a leader to protect them; and they had found one ready to their hand. But the people, when they had the opportunity, would sweep into outer darkness those who, professing democracy, had betrayed them.*

As it turned out, when they had the chance in an election less than a year later, in April 1910, the people did sweep Deakin into the outer darkness. In Australia's first two-party election, the voters gave Labor an absolute majority in both houses. Labor people cheered Fisher when he left Brisbane on the Sydney Express. He was cheered again when he arrived the next morning, then cheered again as he left that night with W. M. Hughes and others on the Melbourne Express; he was met at Spencer Street station the next morning by such a large crowd that the police had to make a way for him to get into the car sent by the governor-general. At the Labor Council, which cancelled its ordinary weekly meeting in order to celebrate the win with songs and speeches, one speaker said that never in the history of the civilised world had there been such a victory. Earlier in the same month Labor had won government in South Australia with an absolute majority in the lower house; six months later it won a majority in New South Wales. Labor Parties were also to win office in Perth, in Hobart, and in Brisbane. It seemed likely that Australia would become the first country in the world with politics dominated by parties speaking in the name of the working class.

In the 1910 election the newly-welded Liberal Party had used many rhetorical devices that were now to become familiar. Its leaders attacked *the wildly extravagant schemes of the socialists with their crazy dreams of reconstructing a society on a basis of human equality that never did and never could exist.* In addition to being socialists, the Labor Party were unificationists, *insidiously moving to strike a death blow at the federal principle by crippling and starving the states into submission so that when all legislation was gathered in a centralised bureaucracy, tyranny would rule and freedom would die.* And both socialism and the unificationism came from the way the Labor Party was controlled by *the decisions of a secret caucus. The choice for Australians was whether they would accept the cramping grip of a despotic caucus or trust the free growth of the free parliament of a free nation.* In whispering campaigns, and in specific attacks from the Loyal Orange Lodges and some of the Protestant organisations, Labor was also represented as being disloyal to God, King and Country; its members were irreligious; their defence policy did not take into account helping the Mother Country; and they wanted to destroy the sanctity of marriage.

The Liberal side said all this. And they lost the election. Labor said it wanted constitutional power for *the nationalisation of monopolies as the only practical means of dealing with the great public evils that had become intolerable in our generation. The chief enemies of a fair and reasonable standard of comfort for all men and women workers were the manufacturing combines, the commercial trusts, the financial institutions and the land monopoly and against these every Labor attack was directed. Against Labor every vested interest in the country that dare show its face was distinctly arrayed; the Liberal Party was supported not only by the great daily papers but also by a secret fund set up by the trusts and by the money power that was the real government of Australia. Yet nothing would now halt the tide of reform that carried Labor on.*

The Labor Party said all this. And won.

***

As one looks at the newspaper files one can hear the cheers that followed Andrew Fisher as he left for Spencer Street Station, in the governor-general's car, on his appointment with what was to be a limited destiny. One can also reconstruct some of the hope, simultaneously arrogant and polite, then beginning to move in the Labor Party. Now they could show themselves as the natural party in Australia, the party of the majority of the people, and the party that would decide what politics was to be about. With Deakin in the outer darkness, it might be Labor that would hold and define the middle ground: then, if a rival party wished to compete with Labor, it would have to do so on Labor's terms.

Imagine this by looking at W. M. Hughes, who was to do much to excite those hopes. To begin with, imagine him in the caucus room in parliament house on the Friday when caucus was choosing the cabinet ministers. While all the others go off for a celebratory lunch, Hughes stays in the caucus room with a plate of beef tea, absorbed in the sadness of his digestive organs. At forty-seven, with ears comically big for such a small body, his face is the face of a boy who has dressed himself up in the dark clothes and stiff collar of a man and, to prove it, wears a false moustache with a sinister droop; by putting on a statesman's confident stare, he tries to brazen out this pretence that he has grown up.

He will go on being alone, tired, over-busy, cantankerous, sick. Sometimes he will comfort himself by retreating for a week or two into a 'breakdown'; there will be rumours that he might give it all up for a cushy job. But he will tempt himself back into action and stay busy by enticing himself with that childish playfulness and caprice that political position can offer. For stretches of time he will leave the attorney-general's department to more or less run itself; then, arbitrarily—the more arbitrarily the more memorably—he might butt in...*where's this? what's happened to that?*...giving the illusion that he knows what is going on.

In 1907, he had written a newspaper article showing how a government minister comes to his department each day already a tired man. 'He signs mechanically the documents placed before him. He is too tired to argue, too indifferent to attempt to do so. He goes to a Cabinet meeting. He listens to men as tired as himself speaking about matters of which they know next to nothing, and in turn they listen while he repeats the lessons typed for him by his department.' But Hughes has the itch of a grand politician: as he presides over events he wants to look as if he knows what he is doing, to give meaning to what is happening, to put on a big show that people will remember. Out of this theatricality he generates his power.

The show he begins to put on in 1910 is that of a great reformer. As attorney-general W. M. Hughes presides from time to time over that modern miracle in which a sentence in a party's policy becomes a complexly-drafted parliamentary bill, and in those never ending questions of manipulation and tactics that are the basis of most legal advice he draws on his own experience as a clever union negotiator who has regularly outsmarted both his own members and the owners. But as attorney-general he is also important as the government's most indefatigable political advocate: no matter what comes up, Hughes is in it; as attorney-general he can speak on anything, and he speaks on everything in the great show of establishing Labor as the party of reform and the natural government of Australia.

Part of this is simple illusionism. To some extent all that Labor is doing is to continue acts of nation-creating agreed to by its predecessors. It starts building a transcontinental railway, it institutes uniform postage, it presides over the beginnings of a national navy, a military college and a citizen military force. A foundation stone is laid for the new national capital. A palace is designed for the Australian High Commission in London. But although these acts merely carry on the work of others, Labor carries them out with a pre-emptive enthusiasm, making them its own.

All the rockets and bungers possessed by the opposition and the press are set off against Labor's establishment of Commonwealth of Australia banknotes. Derided as

'Fisher's flimsies' they are lampooned as likely to destroy the whole Australian credit system. But in defending a nation's right to have its own currency, Labor, to its supporters, can show itself as forward-looking. Merely keeping up with technological change can give the same impression: the first telephone exchange opens; a solar observatory is planned for Mount Stromlo; the government buys a motor car.

It is a time of economic growth and increased immigration. Since what people see as prosperity has returned, to its nation-creating acts Labor can afford to add a program of social and economic reform that, to supporters, can seem evidence of a steady progress in Australian democracy, and to opponents a tyrannical and debilitating socialism. It includes establishing the Commonwealth Bank, a land tax, a new program of land reform, invalid pensions, maternity allowances, an extension of old-age pensions, union preference and workers' compensation for Commonwealth employees and extension of the Arbitration Act to include domestic servants, farm labourers and Commonwealth employees. A rumour is spread that one day Labor might be mad enough to suggest that schoolchildren should be given a free lunch.

In a secular age one of the most important rituals can be the passage of paper; the transformation of a bill into a parliamentary act can be a secular substitute for transubstantiation. In the three years of parliament under the Labor Party forty-one Bills became acts—a record that by its number alone was important in symbolising the possibility of rapid change. When in the 1913 election Labor presented this record to the voters it lost the election, but only by one seat; a year later Labor won a double dissolution election with a bigger majority of votes than in 1910. Had it not been for the accidents that lay in waiting, Labor was probably about to establish Australia as the first of the social-democratic nations, a wonder of the world. Labor had taken over from Deakin the rhetoric of fairness and given it extra significance by a greater readiness towards government action and towards income maintenance. A policy of social concern seemed about to become the new normalcy of Australian politics. Instead, from being a 'social laboratory', Australia was to become a laggard: there would not be even widows' sickness or unemployment benefits until the 1940s; and no effective national health scheme until the 1950s.

***

In the distribution of Deakin's public effects, Fisher had taken over the soft, warm words Deakin had used about fairness and civilisation, and added some of his own; Hughes had taken over Deakin's intelligent concern with rationality and expertness in the conduct of affairs and, because of his greater belief in State intervention, had made this clearer and harder. But W. M. Hughes gained his greatest public effects by two specialities: however desperately enervated he might privately be, in public he would bounce and buzz with energy—he put on a one-man show of the active principle and in Australian politics nothing like it had been seen before—and he was a genius in speaking the language of hatred. He identified an enemy in the trusts and combines, and the identifying of an enemy can be essential to a political cause. These two skills—the talent to appear busy and the talent to project hatred—were to be foremost in Hughes's repertoire when he was later to make a bonfire of what he and Fisher and others had created. But if Hughes had died in 1914, people would have said in later years: 'If only we had a man like W. M. Hughes to lead us now…'

There was opposition from the unions; but social democratic parties can gain political energy from union opposition. To some of the unions, particularly in the Hunter Valley coalfields, the revolutionary syndicalist belief had come from the United States that political action by Labor Parties must fail because the working class and the employer class had nothing in common (an assumption that could seem self-evident in a Hunter Valley pit-top town). It was only by industrial action that the struggle must go on. Then the apocalyptic days would come when the workers combined in one big union; this would give them such great strength that by a single act—a general strike—the workers would bring about their own liberation. When the Hunter Valley miners declared a general strike in November 1909, Hughes put himself at the head of the strike congress. He was presented by the press as a 'temporary dictator of the country', but he was trying to limit the strike, isolate 'the coal barons' and bring public opinion in against them. Times had changed; his tactics were out of date; he failed. For four weeks he was the prime public figure—arguing down rebellious meetings, dealing behind closed doors, giving interviews. Then on 15 December he was defied by the Newcastle strikers: from a hotel balcony he argued at 4,000 of them and, for the first time in his position as Australia's apparently most powerful union leader, he lost the argument. The next day the State government forced through parliament a 'Coercion Act' that gave the government power to gaol anyone connected with the strike and the police power to do almost anything they liked. Intimidated, Hughes announced he would withdraw. 'I will retire, like Cincinnatus to his plough. I will go back to my old brindled cow at Windsor'. He was attacked by the strikers as a rat afraid to go to gaol; he attacked the strikers as having ratted on him by not accepting his advice. (One suggestion was that he had known the Coercion Act was coming, and had gone to Newcastle with the intention of giving the strikers advice that he knew they would not accept, so that he then had a diplomatic reason for abandoning them.)

A militant socialist, Harry Holland, stood against Hughes at the election—the red ribbons of the Socialist Party were seen alongside the red, white and blue of the Liberals and the blue and white of Labor—but he got only a few hundred votes. In the social democratic manner,

Hughes had used the failure of the strike as an argument for political rather than union action: *The day of the coal baron would be ended when the evils of monopoly were destroyed and the community could take control of its own business. Labor was fighting the capitalist too, but it was not fighting him like a bull or a foot. It was fighting him with brains.*

***

Of all W. M. Hughes's public shows, the one he most dominated was the campaign to change the Commonwealth Constitution. When a high court was established in 1903 to interpret the new Constitution its three judges began engaging in an act of creation. In themselves the words of the Constitution were just marks on paper. It was up to the judges to give them a meaning. This act of creation could not, however, appear to be a mere matter of prejudice. How then could the judges give it legitimacy? Holy men were no longer used as judges; when the piece of paper called an act of parliament was offered up to the judges to compare with a piece of paper called a constitution, they would have to declare on its validity with some acceptable substitute for the divine authority that judges used to claim. There were three possibilities—the language of democracy, the language of tradition, or the language of reason. The magic these judges chose was the language of reason, interpreted in an atmosphere of tradition. They would legitimise their decisions by the methods of literary and biblical scholarship, supported by Aristotelian logic, certain conceptual tools and some assumptions as to 'rules'. Since conservatives dominated the early high court, at first completely, then in the ratio three to two, by the techniques of rationality the words of an already restrictive Constitution were given conservative meanings. To the Labor Party, this could seem the principal obstacle to the party's chance of providing future political dominance in

Australia. It was Hughes's task to do something about it.

Hughes had the opportunity to break it, as an attorney-general who had to appoint three new justices; but he failed. Fisher had spoken openly of the need for Labor 'representation' in the high court but this had embarrassed Hughes, who wanted to seem to be playing the game. He faced the problem that, in a profession so conservative, a Labor judge could seem a 'political appointment' whereas a conservative judge could seem 'impartial'. Hughes tried a compromise: his list contained a conventional nominee; a nonentity; and a radical liberal. The uproar from the Sydney and Melbourne barristers at once led the radical liberal to jump out of the ring. The game Hughes was playing was one whose rules were set by Labor's opponents.

Hughes's way out was to keep on fighting referendum campaigns until he won. After the 1910 election he organised his first referendum, held in 1911. It was the first of the many national campaigns in which for the next ten years he would spend such a large proportion of his life as a minister. (The same voice; the same gestures; but different arguments.) He was acting prime minister (Fisher had gone off to London for King George's crowning) but for seven weeks his main preoccupation was to travel over five states, speaking from platforms in city town halls and country schools of arts. On the powers sought over trade and commerce he would say that *to assert that the national government must not have control of the well-spring from which all must perforce drink or die was to reduce the national government to a condition of impotence and to grievously impair the welfare of every individual in the community*. On the powers sought over labour and employment he would say that there *could be no democratic government, if industry was not to be controlled and systematised in a sane, beneficent and effective fashion for the benefit of the whole community*. On the powers sought over corporations and the power to nationalise monopolies he would say that *one of the chief causes of the increased cost of living was the existence of combines and trusts which fixed prices to suit themselves and nobody else. Were we to live and work and carry on industrial organisation operations for the benefit of a few persons, or for the benefit of the whole people?*

It was his greatest defeat. Seven weeks of train travel and town halls, banners and cheers, and the little man whose talking from streetcorners and hotel balconies and local halls, at hundreds of political rallies and union meetings, had usually preceded victory, had now produced a defeat: less than 40% of voters voted 'Yes'. But he began planning the next referendum, presenting much the same questions, but more appealingly, and when two years later he had his next go, almost 50% of the voters voted 'Yes'. If the accidents of war had not been waiting ahead, at the next referendum he would probably have gained his victory.

Meanwhile Hughes had bought himself a motor car, beginning a career as one of Australia's most dangerous drivers, as he was later to develop a career as one of its most erratic golfers; and Fisher, who quietly kept a keen, shrewd eye on his own private affairs, handling his money cleverly, bought a big house in a garden so large that when Hughes paid his first visit, he jokingly brought a pocket compass. Some of the Labor men rejected invitations to government house functions; Hughes enjoyed them. The funny windbag of 'Oleander Lodge' was becoming the amusing anecdotalist of government house levees. He still had only one intimate friend in the Labor Party, but colleagues were finding him easier to get on with.

Hughes had been using his daughter Ethel, now aged twenty-two, to act as hostess as well as run the house, but in June 1911 he made a new arrangement. At a time when he was acting prime minister, he married, quietly, in a church at South Yarra, Mary Campbell, a squatter's daughter. She built a new life around him; one in which there was less room for old associates.

Chapter 3

Billy Hughes, Patriot

Not long before Will Hughes started his shop in Balmain—in the year that celebrated the hundredth anniversary of the storming of the Bastille—the second International Working Men's Association was launched at a congress in Paris, in a hall rich with red cloth and red flags, and with gold letters above the rostrum proclaiming WORKING MEN OF ALL COUNTRIES, UNITE! By 1914, at a congress of the Second International there could have been delegates from as many as twenty-five nations; in these nations several million people belonged to the socialist parties and there were several hundred socialist members of parliament. As the congresses of the Second International met, and saw their growing strength, the first worldwide anti-war movement developed, with the slogan 'War on War!'. At the congress, and at meetings of the executive bureau, delegates spoke of how international working class action could prevent war. In the minutes book was a resolution that even if war did break out it was the workers' duty *to intervene in favour of its speedy termination, and with all their powers to utilize the economic and political crisis created by the war to rouse the masses and thereby to hasten the downfall of capitalist class rule.*

There had been much debate on how working-class action might prevent a war—a general strike? mass uprisings?—and when the executive bureau of the International met in the Hall of the People in Brussels at the end of July 1914, that debate was resumed. The delegates from Austria-Hungary, whose government had already announced its ultimatum to Serbia, saw no hope. ('Parliament is suspended. Public meetings are prohibited. Anyone who resists mobilisation will be hanged'.) But others were optimistic that there would not be a general war. Keir Hardie, from Britain, saw British intervention as 'quite out of the question'; Jaures, the French delegate said 'I assure you, the French government wants peace'. Hugo Haase, the German delegate, claimed The Kaiser was against the war, not for humanitarian reasons but simply from fear'. At the great open-air rally with which the bureau's conference ended, there were mass chants of the slogan 'War on War!' The delegates went away to organise.

The next day hundreds of thousands of Germans held peace demonstrations, with twenty-seven rallies in Berlin alone. That was the day Austria declared war on Russia. The next day there were many huge peace demonstrations in the main towns of Great Britain. Two days later the German and French members of parliament voted for war credits. That was the end of the Second International.

In Australia as in other countries some of the small socialist groups maintained faith in the International's ideals: It was a wicked and unnecessary war, directly the result of a world-wide system of capitalist exploitation that was striving to get absolute control of Australia, as it was doing elsewhere. But at the beginning only the fringe of the labour movement spoke this language; and only a handful of Labor MPs plainly spoke of any doubts. Without hesitation the leaders of the Labor Party committed men to slaughter.

With cables about mobilisations, ultimatums and declarations of war appearing in the Australian newspapers and coinciding with the beginning of a national election campaign, Labor strategy was to outshout the Liberals in loyalist rhetoric. On 31 July Fisher, now leader of the opposition, and Cook, now Liberal prime minister, played two phrases tested in the rhetoric of Australia's empire loyalty. Cook proclaimed that *when the Empire was at war, Australia was at war.* On the same night, in the Victorian Western District, Fisher said that *Australia would help and defend the Mother Country to its last man and its last shilling.* But several days later Hughes, seeking a part for Australia *worthy of the traditions and spirit of our race,* suggested the election be called off to allow the *warring factions to join hands in the gravest crisis of our history.* Cook rejected this *very flimsy and transparent screen behind which Labor has been seeking to hide its naked partisanship,* but he had lost the initiative, and his appeal to voters *not to change the pilot, to stay with the Liberals with their agelong experience rather than Labor with its unproved panaceas* gave Labor another initiative: *in such a dark hour, when the very existence of the Empire and the Commonwealth hangs in the balance the reins of government should be entrusted to the Labor men who had proved their capacity, and in time of peace foresaw and prepared for war.* At the end of the campaign when the newspapers let out their hunting cries, the Hobart *Mercury*—fearing that if Sydney were invaded, under a Labor government it might become a Commune like Paris in 1871—asked if *we should have men in power who, if not Communists themselves, were half-hearted in supporting the Old Country* but the Brisbane *Worker* proclaimed *that just as Australian Labor had shown the world many object lessons in the way of standing shoulder to shoulder in time of trouble, now Australian Labor would stand shoulder to shoulder with old England in this her hour of storm and stress.*

The position in Australia would have been beyond the imagination of European socialists. Even after their collapse in August 1914, the socialist parties in Europe, although they voted support for the war, still saw themselves as outside the state apparatus. In Australia (in an election in which both contesting parties were led by former miners) Labor had successfully promoted itself over its opponents as the party for running a war, and by the middle of September it had taken over the government.

With Fisher as prime minister, imagine W. M. Hughes, again attorney-general and now also deputy leader of the party, aged fifty-two, grey-haired and grey-moustached, his face seamed and wrinkled, arriving in his motor car at the attorney-general's department and settling into his chair to read the latest regulations drafted under the War Precautions Act—regulations about newspaper censorship, or the offence of encouraging disloyalty to the British Empire, or alien internment camps. Then recall the clean-shaven thirty-two-year-old Will Hughes arriving after his penny tram ride at the New South Wales parliament in 1894 to make a speech saying that Australia needed no armies at all because it was 10,000 miles from danger. Or even the W. M. Hughes of several years before, prophet of a simple, democratic militia and a citizen navy, to be used only in the defence of Australia.

In its turmoil, the hurricane of the new imperialism has whirled away Hughes, along with tens of millions of others who are caught up in a depravity that will last for two generations, sometimes raging with an obliterative force. Crazed with metaphors of blood, Hughes is to be one of the orators of this depravity.

Australia was entering into its predicted savage destiny. In 1852 in his book *Freedom and Independence for the Golden Lands of Australia*, the crackpot republican patriot John Dunmore Lang had forecast that so far from being the case that loyalty to Britain would save Australia, it was only this loyalty that could drag into danger a country so remote from the centres of power. Now his prophecy had come true. If the romantic dream of the pragmatists had been reality and if Australians had been able to strip away sentiment until they could see nothing but their own material self-interest what Dunmore Lang had forecast would have seemed clear enough: Australia would be better off out of the empire, even if still prudently friendly with it; and it would have seemed clear to an independent Australia in 1914 that there was no material self-interest in the war for Australians, except to make money out of it as a neutral. If at some stage calculated self-interest did suggest participation, that could have been kept late, and inexpensive in money and lives. But by 1914, prevailing conceptions of both national self-interest and national honour (which usually ride together because humans want to be proud of what they do) both pointed straight to the slaughterhouse. Those Australians who defined themselves with such vanity and such calculation as part of 'the British race', endorsed sentences of death, mutilation or degradation on tens of thousands of their young.

***

The young were happy, at first in the confident spirit of the military expeditions that had already gone to New Zealand, to the Sudan, to South Africa and to China to suppress anti-imperial uprisings. And since throughout the European nations national honour was beginning to be attached to sporting teams and sporting heroes, among the bugles and trumpets and the more traditional patriotic speeches there were appeals to the sporting spirit. Sending off 20,000 men to what would probably be a short war could be an even more convincing demonstration of Australian worth than a cricket or tennis team or a sculling or boxing champion. It would show how, in the words of a hit song written before the first contingent left, 'Australia will be there'. It was an era of tales of pluck and derring-do, of flags, banners, uniforms, brass bands, lively patriotic songs, with exemplary stories of colonialism's saints and martyrs. And to these were added, as had happened similarly in the United States with the 'cowboy', the local yarns of the unique adventurousness and manliness of the Australian 'bushmen'. The war would demonstrate not only Australians' sporting prowess: it would demonstrate their rural virtue.

Above the volunteers as they marched off behind their bands and their banners there was also the black rhetoric, streaked with scarlet, of the official funerary orators, calling for purification through self sacrifice in bearing the burden of maintaining a Christian civilisation that had fallen uniquely on 'the British race'. But the motives of men who fight in armies may be quite different from the official rhetoric that, from above, urges them on. To many ordinary Australians this was simply overblown Pommy talk, but in such a human stampede those on the official platforms have the first option to declare what it has all been about, and they can put their rivals in gaol. Hughes was to be pre-eminent both as gaoler and as funerary orator.

For the first year of the war, he was more gaoler than orator. While other ministers presided over the collecting of recruits at emergency camps on the racecourses, the clothing of them in uniforms of pure Australian wool, the paying of them at a rate criticised by King George as too much for a soldier, the transporting of them overseas, the setting up of factories to equip them and the financing of all this unusual expense, Hughes's initial share in the playfulness of war was to fight 'the enemy within the gates'. As attorney-general he was central to the State's apparatus of power; he read the coercive regulations as they were drafted, and lived in the world of censorship, internments, and arrests.

But by granting him a holiday from tradition, war had also allowed him to break some of the old constraints, and imagine what state socialism might have been like. When wheat ships were lacking, he began organising a 'freight pool' of shipping; when he read in a magazine article how three Frankfurt companies controlled a large part of the world's trade in base metals through variously named dummy companies in Britain, North America, Africa and Australia (the Australian company was blandly called the 'Australian Metal Company') he was able to do what he had spoken of so often from so many town hall platforms and hotel balconies: he busted a combine. With a mixture of acts of parliament, special regulations, law court actions, raids on company offices, threats, abuse and sweet talk, he broke up the German control of base metals in Australia and caused to be set up in its place Australian institutions for refining and marketing metals. He also had the manager of the Australian Metal Company arrested, and put him in an internment camp.

***

Although Hughes was impatient with him, and probably jealous of him, Andrew Fisher was proving a good wartime prime minister. He was a man with deadening powers of reassurance. With his tall, upright bearing, his broad forehead, his steady gaze and his square jaw, he had the appearance of a 'Christian soldier' in a schoolboys' annual rather than that of a mad socialist. He could be moved to firmness: as befitted a Labor man, he got on well with his staff and was open and democratic in his manner— anyone who wished might call him 'Andy'—but as a miner who had married a mine manager's daughter he was sensitive to snubs, and if he sensed one, would play the prime minister. His greatest talent was his lack of obvious talent: because he was so reassuringly ordinary there was general admiration for his integrity. He did not arouse enthusiasm but (except perhaps for Hughes) he did not arouse envy or enmity.

At the same time reticent and friendly, cautious and vehement, stubborn and moderate, he usually cleared the papers on his desk; he had some eye for detail and at least a recognition of the need for decision. Army camps were constructed to replace the racecourse improvisations; government factories (seen as 'socialistic' by some opponents) produced uniforms, cordite, rifles and bayonets, harness; shell factories were set up to operate when the new Broken Hill Proprietary plant at Newcastle began producing steel; new methods (attacked as 'class taxation') were devised for raising public money.

And if part of the test of a wartime leader are the tests of humanity and prudence, Fisher can be seen as exceptionally able. In presiding over the assembling of the Australian divisions and their reinforcement, he was not over-zealous. He allowed men to volunteer, but he did not urge them to do so. Now that Fisher had won the election, he was not pressing out the last man and the last shilling. He was not even ready to appoint a director-general of recruiting, nor to set up a propaganda drive to entice men into battle. At the end of 1914 he said there would be no special effort to obtain recruits; six months later all he would say was that a young man who felt like fighting should see the recruiting sergeant. When a special citizens' recruiting drive was launched in Victoria he refused to adjourn parliament to allow members to take part in it. When the new Universal Service League was set up in September, with the Catholic Archbishop of Sydney as a vice-president, it was supported by that same Holman, now premier of New South Wales, who used to talk socialism and solidarity in Hughes's shop at Balmain, but Fisher publicly announced that he was irrevocably opposed to conscription, as, he was sure, were his colleagues; privately, he thought that if conscription were introduced it would lead to open revolt, at least in Queensland. Fisher was concerned with keeping the labour movement's support for the moderate war program already existing. In caucus a 'torpedo brigade' was trying to sink existing compromises by demanding a greater effort for socialist objectives; one MP had resigned from the Labor Party because it had abandoned its social reform program; some Labor speakers publicly attacked what they saw as the party's over-concentration on the war and, in effect, the war itself. When parliamentary opponents criticised Fisher on this, demanding that speakers be treated as traitors, Fisher protected them with an opaque wordiness. As a wartime prime minister he was no more murderous than was needed for him to stay in position; and understanding the limits of his power he could see that a more adventurous policy would fail. His prudence and political skill were the model of all that Hughes lacked.

But like all the moderate men in positions of power in any of the nations fighting in the war, Fisher was to be lost in the tide.

***

For Australians the tide began to sweep on the morning of 25 April 1915. By about 2.30 on that morning the soldiers who were to be the covering force for the Australian landing on the Gallipoli peninsula had shuffled down the sides of their transports into three dozen rowing boats, thirty or forty to a boat. Half an hour later, the moon set. At 3.30 the boats moved off, in batches of three, towed for an hour by steamboats through a darkness in which all that could be heard was the rustle of satin-black water and the pulsing and hissing of engines. When the faint outlines of the shore showed up in the first pale light, the boats were cast off. There was the soft swish of muffled oars...a light flared, bright yellow...a man's figure was outlined on a ridge...bullets flipped into the sea... the wounded moaned as they slid to the bottoms of the boats...Sparks flew against the shingles as men ran over the beach to the cover of a sandy bank; blood dripped on the sand. According to orders the men were now supposed to slip off their packs and rush across 200 metres of open land to the first ridge. But there was no open land: a high, rugged slope pressed down on them. They had landed on the wrong beach.

Gravelly sand slipped under boots and prickly bushes tore at uniforms as they rushed the slope, pulling themselves up the steeper parts by grasping at the roots and tough branches of the scrub. In a confusion of small ridges, and dry gravelly gullies they found a bushy ridge on a plateau with two gullies cutting into it and a maze of ridges. Here they sorted themselves out, dug rifle pits, formed up. Other waves of troops moved into empty scrub, were stopped by cliffs, clambered along ridges, were blocked in gullies. Men paused when they shouldn't have, gave orders that made no sense. The ridge they had been ordered to seize remained dark, distant and quiet. Then they met the disasters of Turkish shells and bullets. By midnight dismal rain was falling; hundreds of stragglers and thousands of wounded had retreated to the beach; ahead, in the dark, a 'front' was forming as men, having scoured the slopes for picks and shovels, began to dig. In a headquarters made of a few sandbags and a strip of canvas, the generals waited for news to come that the commander-in-chief in his battleship had agreed that they should evacuate.

No significant advance was to be made on what had been seized on the first day—the most that was occupied was about three square miles of the enemy's dust and gravel and furze and sand. Men sat among the roots and the dirt of the firing trenches and sniped at the Turks, or tried to tunnel under Turkish trenches; sometimes they were slaughtered in a failed offensive; sometimes they slaughtered Turks in a failed counter-offensive. They ate and slept on the sides of valleys in holes in the ground or in little humpies of canvas, blankets and tin drums; they swam on the beach they had re-named Anzac, after themselves. As well as the flies and fleas and lice and the diarrhoea and dysentery bacteria, a legend began to spread. On mail days the men could read about how they had created the Australian nation.

Anzac was an act of instant myth. For several days after the landing all there was to read in the Australian newspapers were casualty lists and cables of congratulations from big shots, with no indication of why the men were dying, or why they were being congratulated for doing so, but on 8 May when a despatch from an English war correspondent was published making an heroic tale of the landing, Australians recognised the sign they had been waiting for: *In one moment Australia had stepped into the worldwide arena in the full stature of great manhood and now took its place among the nations.* Such phrases had been ready for a generation or more.

Now it could seem true. Out of a failed adventure Australia was to be defined as a nation created by what was seen as military virtue.

But among those who supported the war, there were doubters. For those educated Australians who saw human excellence as a question of keeping up with the British, Australia could *never* come of age. When the boys had marched off to the troopships in what were seen as ill-fitting and unmilitary uniforms, some culture-bearers had doubted whether such rough stuff could be made trim enough for anything more important than lines of communication work; and when the Anzac reports came in—although it was impressive that the first of them was from an Englishman—they doubted the reports. And subversively many of the soldiers themselves were uneasy about the way they were being praised. They made fun of 'the jingo writers' and their phrases...*deathless heroes...lasting glory... gallant guardians of Britain's honoured name*. Contrasting themselves with the *chooms* and their *toff* officers, the soldiers preferred the laconic and comradely style of *cobbers* and *mates*. They protected their identity by glorying in many of those key words and anecdotes that had been given distinctive tang by the old lags, the currency lads, the diggers, the bushmen and the larrikins, and, in an act of collective creation, they gave the Anzac legend a folk meaning as well as a chauvinist one, interpreting into it ideals of casualness, fraternity and scepticism.

To correct this, what was needed was the gloomy imperial melodrama of the funeral orators. The most notable of these professional mourners, reducing the Anzacs to the safe clichés of routine imperial rhetoric, was to be Hughes. Even as a union leader and a Labor Party leader, he had never used the homely language of Australian folk democracy; nor did he do so now. He did not speak of the Anzacs in their own language. But he rose on the fame of the Anzacs. Now it was time for him to become prime minister.

***

Hughes forced Fisher's resignation, but it was the resignation of a man who could feel, as if he were suffering them in his own body, the great strains that were now testing the labour movement.

In the manner of politics, the precipitating incident that pushed Fisher out was trivial. Fisher promises Cook, as leader of the opposition, that a certain parliamentary bill will be adjourned for a fortnight. The next week, in Fisher's absence, Hughes brings the bill on. Cook protests. Fisher's honour is impugned. His resentment of years of Hughes's unreliable pushiness overwhelms him. His forthrightness breaks through his reticence and he threatens Hughes: he will never work with him again. The high commissionership in London is vacant: Hughes can resign, go to London and become high commissioner. But within Hughes's wrinkled little body there is more venom, more ambition, more determined self-belief, more energy, than is left inside the tallness and handsomeness of Andy Fisher. Hughes says he won't go, and his bluff wins. Fisher gives in, and sends himself to London, leaving behind the story that he is tired and in ill health. He will now serve under Hughes unhappily.

On 27 October 1915 Hughes becomes prime minister of Australia.

***

By the particular test of 1915, he still seemed a Labor stalwart, in that he remained a *fighter for the working class against the greed of the war profiteers*. He was one of those who had made it clear that merely because there was a war was no reason for the workers to suffer. The war had immediately thrown thousands of Australians out of work—there were demonstrations against unemployment as early as December 1914—and when in 1915, prices increased at a time when many wages were still frozen, Hughes had agreed with those who saw it as the work of 'profiteering bandits'. To the irritation of the controlling Holman faction in New South Wales, he had turned up as a rank-and-file delegate at the New South Wales Labor Party conference in April (he was there as president of the Carters' union, not as attorney-general) and had helped manoeuvre support for a referendum that would have given the national government, amongst other things, power to fix prices. In the voting to choose New South Wales delegates to the newly-created federal executive, and to the Labor Party's interstate conference in May Hughes had topped the list, and at the interstate conference, when it was held, it was Hughes who had framed a motion calling for a referendum to give the national government power to fix prices and make bulk purchases of commodities; despite protests from two State Labor governments (who wanted to protect State rights) the motion had got through.

In June Hughes had been up on his feet in the house of representatives, doing again what he had already done so well—introducing a bill to hold a referendum to give the national government greater powers—and jeering so successfully at an opposition that attacked the bill as a party measure, unpatriotic in wartime, that the whole opposition had walked out. No matter. Polling day was set for 11 December.

Holman was already in danger from the New South Wales party machine, partly from those militant and increasingly syndicalist unions whose leaders saw him as a lapsed socialist and a warmonger, and partly from the Australian Workers' Union whose leaders saw him as even better at stacking conferences than they were, but when Hughes began attacking the profiteering bandits a wave of enthusiasm went through most of the labour movement. He was speaking labour language. A fighting Labor Party had just won the Queensland elections, and here was Hughes, back on the spruiking box, although he was now prime minister. Labor had reached the high tide mark of its potential in Australia.

When he was still prime minister, Andrew Fisher had said that nothing short of an earthquake would prevent the prices referendum. The earthquake now happened. Throughout the nation, business interests and newspapers campaigned against holding the referendum and, fighting the same fight, the Liberals attacked it as devisive, promoting national division; the Australian Women's National League, a conservative organisation, presented a petition against the bill, with 55,000 signatures; the State premiers, including Labor premiers, brought pressure. As the new prime minister, Hughes found this campaign more significant than the labour movement's wishes. He gave in.

Using the subterfuge of asking the States to refer powers, he abandoned the referendum off his own bat, without a word to any labour organisation, except, retrospectively, to a meeting of the parliamentary caucus, which was called without notice and asked to give its approval an hour before a statement was due in parliament. By this act he let loose in the labour movement all the suspicions that would for the rest of his life be attached to anything he did. So in 1915 Hughes abandoned a referendum which would have divided the nation in a way that would have separated him from his political enemies; in 1916 he was to call a referendum, on conscription, that would divide the nation in a way that would separate him from his political friends.

This was the Labor Party's first significant surrender to a campaign from the business companies and their allies. At a time when business as a whole seems challenged and business people unite, they can threaten a government in ways unavailable to the trades unions. For the whole range of unions to maintain industrial action for even a short time is so rare that if it does happen, it is called a revolution, but men who control business can summon powerful antes to take over most of the public conduct of their case, so that it seems in the national interest.

However union leaders jilted by a Labor government

can dream of one terrible revenge—one they can take only against a Labor government—that of combining their strength in the Labor Party to shake a government to bits. Sometimes this dream takes flesh. Any Labor leader must take this melodramatic possibility into account. It is one of the many limitations of office and there are equal, if less visible, restraints on Labor's political opponents. Hughes, who had been part of such a process in the 1890s as a candidate of the Solidarity Labor Party against the Bogus Labor Party, and who had kept a tough trades-union base, now acted like a man in a new dream.

A few days after his sudden and painful alienation of the labour movement he committed himself to another act of devious recklessness: on 11 November he told the caucus and, later in the day, parliament that he was going to London. He suggested that he had received a special invitation to a conference there, but in fact he hadn't: there was nothing more than a general invitation to colonial prime ministers to drop in some time, unenthusiastically repeated to Hughes when he asked the governor-general to sound out the colonial office. His fancy was bewitched by visions of London and the importance of his going there, although Fisher had only just arrived in London and might have been expected to get a few things done. Yet this was a period when, as a result of Hughes's abandoning the referendum, even the conservative unions were talking of disciplining their 'parliamentary delegates'—in the very words used by Hughes and Holman when, outsiders looking in, they preached working-class solidarity against Labor MPs cut off from their party base. A few days before he sailed he was censured by the federal executive. He bluffed it out: by threatening to resign, he forced them to rescind their censure. After less than three months as prime minister Hughes had already played a prime minister's last card.

He stayed away for six months.

***

25 April 1916, the first Anzac Day—in London it is a sunny spring. Australian and New Zealand troops march behind two bands from Waterloo Station to Westminster Abbey for an Anzac Day service, at which the souvenir of the commemoration is dominated by a photograph of General Birdwood, the British commander of the Anzacs (described on the souvenir as 'soul of Anzac') with photographs of King George and Queen Mary on either side. All three, along with other British notables, are at the service in Westminster Abbey. Then, after a lunch at the Hotel Cecil, Hughes's turn comes: from the stage of Her Majesty's theatre he tells the Australian soldiers *their deeds had won them a place in the Temple of the Immortals. The world had hailed them as heroes. On the shining wings of their glorious valour they had inspired us to a newer and better and nobler concept of life; and the deathless deeds of the valiant dead would yet be sung in sagas to generations of Australians to the end of time. The story of the Gallipoli campaign had shown that through self-sacrifice alone could men or a nation be saved. And since it had evoked this pure and noble spirit, who should say that this dreadful war was wholly evil now that in a world saturated with a lust of material things came the sweet, purifying breath of self sacrifice?*

With his wife, the squatter's daughter, beside him, and Helen, their recently-born baby, to delight him—he was to show to her a devoted love he could find for no other fellow creature—Hughes was being lionised. He had been taken up by groups of British businessmen, who admired his bluntness in describing the war as a trade war, and therefore all the better for winning since there would be rich gains for the victors; he had also been taken up by Lord Milner, a gentleman conspirator who, with his 'Round Table' of devotees, was a specialist in endearing colonials to the empire's cause, and to a lesser extent by Lord Northcliffe, the prototype press baron, who assumed the right to push British politics into his own pattern, partly by personal intrigue and private blackmail, partly by the public bullying of his newspapers. For the months he spent in Britain Hughes was floated on a cloud of high prestige: not only did he stay with King George at Windsor Castle, dine with the Archbishop of Canterbury at Lambeth Palace, and see the commander-in-chief at general headquarters; for a season he was entertained almost daily, at public receptions or private dinners; he was given the freedom of the cities of London, Manchester, Birmingham, York, Sheffield, Cardiff, Bristol and Edinburgh; universities gave him honorary doctorates; King George made him a privy councillor; and the newspapers projected him as a world figure.

In particular, with the clever young Australian journalist Keith Murdoch helping him with contacts and publicity, Hughes made speeches. The voice that had rasped over the produce stores and wharves of Sydney's waterfront now sounded in guild halls, city halls, university halls, smart restaurants and the dining rooms of gentlemen's clubs and fashionable hotels. Hughes was being used by Milner in his latest conspiracy—an attempt to replace Asquith as prime minister. When he was put on his speech-making circuit, he was given a role in the developing Wake-Up-England campaign that was to provide background clamour to the replacement of Asquith by Lloyd George. Perhaps Hughes saw the laconic Asquith as a gentlemanly counterpart to the stolid Andy Fisher, and David Lloyd George as the W. M. Hughes of Britain. Whatever he thought, as part of one of those political rushes that can mistake noise and mere busyness for effective action, and knowing nothing of Asquith's private toughness and finesse, Hughes saw Asquith as someone 'temperamentally unfitted to lead the empire in war. He looked upon action as a kind of disease. He was perhaps too perfectly civilised.' The effect of Hughes's speeches was that a colonial prime minister was campaigning in Britain against the British prime minister. Hughes later boasted that without his help, Lloyd George would never have dared supplant Asquith, but he gave himself too much initiative. To both Milner, whose group met every Monday for dinner to contrive Asquith's downfall, and to Northcliffe, who was trying to bully Asquith out of the prime ministership, Hughes was someone whom it was convenient to use. His image floated from the guildhalls and palaces of Britain across the Channel into the French newspapers, where he was praised ('a magnificent campaign for economic defence against Germany'…'he may be considered to represent the real views of England') and the German newspapers, where he was attacked ('the darling of the imperialists and the jingo agitators, who make far-reaching demands with very little intelligence… 'it makes almost a grotesque effect, and shows the complete helplessness of England's cause that a man from the antipodes gifted with a loud voice is held up as the saviour of the British Empire'). In Australia, his speeches were printed with enthusiasm; like that of the Anzacs, Hughes's fame was a token that Australia had come of age.

In the rhetorical world of Hughes's speeches, *through policies of drift in the prosaic days of peace Britain had stood on the crumbling edge of destruction, slumbering on peacefully, relying upon providence, managing somehow or other to muddle through. Even in this great crisis, with the civilised world locked in death grips with the greatest enemy that had appeared, we in this happy land had still been peacefully pursuing the even tenor of our way. It needed the Celtic imagination* (of Hughes and Lloyd George?) *to see the blood stained horrors of war. There was between the ideals of Britain and Germany a gulf as wide as divides heaven from hell, right from wrong. Yet there were men who spoke of peace. What a confession of decadent futility! Was it nothing to these men that this military despotism which had terrified the world for forty years, should stand now upon the very entrails of Belgium, nothing that she should stand among the outraged women and murdered children; that she should roam the seas as a bloody-minded pirate? Everything was at stake—spiritual, moral and material—for which we as a people stood.*

Yet this war which had plunged civilisation into an inferno, which had saturated the earth with the blood of our sons, had welded the scattered nations of our Empire into one united people. We remained full of the valour of our ancient race and we would not only emerge triumphant in this great struggle, but we would be purged of dross and purified by the spirit of self sacrifice. This war had saved the British Empire from moral—aye, and physical—degeneration and decay. The British race had found its soul.

It was to her organisation that Germany owed her tremendous strength; there was one leader and all men followed him; the efforts of every individual were systematised; every resource of science, every mechanical invention, had been organised; every need of the people was known; every means to supply it was exploited. Nothing short of a resolution as determined as Germany's, an organisation as complete as Germany's would enable us to conquer in the fields both of battle and of trade. We should all vow to regard this great work of national organisation as a sacred duty. Mr Lloyd George had given the very operation by which this war could be won—action, action, action. We stood literally on the crumbling edge of destruction. Now, thanks to Mr Lloyd George's gargantuan labours and to the glorious spirit of our people we might venture to breathe more easily.

Three Hughes books (all prompted by Murdoch) were published in London in 1916. In a foreword to one of them, a collection of Hughes's speeches, Lloyd George said: 'No public speeches of modern times have made such an impression on the British public' and of the two books that others had written about Hughes one was subtitled *The Man of the Hour* and the other *The Strong Man of Australia*. Over a three-week period when he was ill, there were daily health bulletins in *The Times*. When Asquith showed disinclination to invite Hughes to an economic conference in Paris, the French as well as the British papers attacked Asquith and King George intervened to say that Hughes should go to Paris.

For the six months Hughes was away from Australia he paid some attention to Australian affairs—his most notable adventure was the purchase for Australia of a merchant marine, carried out in a daring Hughes coup, when, despite British protests and threats to requisition the ships back, he bought fifteen tramp steamers (at six times their original cost) on a bank overdraft—but what dominated these six months—apart from sickness—was speech-making. Drafts would be dictated; typescripts might be worked over several more times; key passages might be rehearsed; then off Hughes would go to whatever grand function it was with a fair copy, typed and ready to read. In speaking, he would employ those tricks of voice and gesture he first cultivated in himself in the shop at Beattie Street; and he would often pause for the applause that the young Balmain elocutionist must have craved.

***

Twelve days before Hughes arrived back in Australia the 5th Australian Division was tossed into battle, and shattered after a night's fighting. The British were trying diversionary tricks north of the area where the Somme offensive had begun seventeen days before, and with losses of 100,000 there was already some of the fearsome shape of that meticulously stubborn tragedy. Out of one of these diversions a British corps commander developed a spruce ambition: he wanted to tidy up his front line near the village of Fromelles. The day before the attack was due a staff officer from GHQ tried to talk him out of his neatness, but the general said cancellation of his plans would be bad for the troops' morale.

The attack began at 6 p.m. at the end of a bright summer day—and after a four-day bombardment that had warned the Germans that something might be coming. Tidiness at once fell into fiasco. In one section, scattered parties of Australians had taken over the German front and in the haze of smoke and dust were looking for the 'third line' they were to seize and hold. There wasn't one. Isolated from each other, they filled sandbags with mud and made do with fortified posts in some of the ditches. But in the smoke to the right, the Australians had been shot down in a wrecked orchard, and at dusk it was the Germans who attacked—from both flanks—moving in behind the Australians, and in a second assault, after midnight, they fought into even stronger positions. In the mists of dawn they attacked the Australians from the rear. For the next four hours parties of Australians desperately bombed and shot their way through the surrounding Germans back to where they had started. As rolls were called in trenches packed with wounded, dying and dead the 5th Australian Division found that in one night it had lost 5,533 men. It could not fight again for several months.

Beginning three days later, for seven weeks, amongst the rubble of Pozieres village and the shredded tree stumps of Mouquet Farm, three other Australian divisions became one of the main agents of a new GHQ plan, officially named 'methodical progress'. In turn, each division was methodically thrown against mounds of smoking rubble and stretches of reeking mud: it would be methodically mutilated, methodically withdrawn, methodically patched up, and methodically thrown back again. They lost 23,000 men. In the last letter before his death, a brave lieutenant wrote of the 'murder' of his friends 'through the incompetence, callousness and personal vanity of those high in authority'. Another officer wrote: 'We have just come out of a place so terrible that a raving lunatic could never imagine the horror of the last thirteen days'. The shambling mile-long front of this disaster sopped up more Australian blood than any other place on earth.

***

From his landing at Perth on 31 July Hughes received the greatest conquering hero's welcome Australia had seen. In each of the capital cities, Perth, Adelaide and

Melbourne, the authorities put him on the roof of an automobile so that enormous crowds could look at him and they drove him to the largest hall so that enormous crowds could hear him. At every stop on the train journey crowds went to the station to cheer and sing 'God Save the King' and 'Home Sweet Home'; and just as the voters of Darling Harbour used to express the poignancy they found in the contrast between his smallness and his high promise by speaking proudly of 'little Willie', Australians everywhere could now take pride in him as 'Billy Hughes'. There began that tradition that lasted until he died in which any Australian who saw Hughes in the street could demonstrate affection for Australian democracy by calling out 'Hello, Billy'.

In the legendary form in which they imagined him, Billy Hughes did not exist. But people needed him. So they invented him. He seemed to be a statesman who had gained a name for Australia overseas. And he seemed to be a man of genius who knew how to win the war.

In fact, Hughes was an incompetent wartime prime minister. In the Napoleonic style of governing by relying on sudden well-organised surprise attacks, he was able to bring off successful *coups,* as he did in breaking the German metals combine, or, more questionably, in buying a merchant marine of fifteen overpriced freighters. He also could sometimes successfully rely on good work by staff so that he could put on a show of doing everything himself: in particular, he had a clever (and loyal) solicitor-general who knew how to use government regulations to cut corners, or to coerce recalcitrants; and he had chosen some clever men in a few other fields, particularly in the pooling arrangements for selling commodities. In the manner of a politician, he could sound as if he knew what he was talking about: he was a bold master of briefs, and he had learned the tricks of appearing to have absorbed detail. He was a great craftsman in the skills of stubbornness and of the dramatic intervention. (A French journalist described him at the conference in Paris: *frail, narrow-*

shouldered, stooped, with the long, metallic face, seamed with lines, of a Breton peasant, at first he sits doubled up like a spider and lets others talk; already he has been forgotten by the other speakers; but suddenly he straightens out, darts forward his thin arms and the double trident of stretched out fingers, and cuts through the flabbiness of the discussion with a word.) Like many successful politicians, he was an artist in secretiveness *(He has all the arts of a crab,* said Munro-Ferguson, the governor-general, *and when he does not wish to be drawn, he withdraws within the impenetrable shell of his designs).* He was also skilled at subterfuge and deceit, as politicians often are, and in the arts of candour as well; he could burst out with a frankness, or what passed for it, which was likely to induce the sympathetic warmth that politicians need to cuddle up against. (In one of his crises he rang Munro-Ferguson at Admiralty House, in Sydney, at 11 o'clock at night and said he wanted a talk; the governor-general dressed, crossed to Circular Quay in a launch, then sat in a taxi while Hughes discussed his problems.) Also like many a successful politician, he could be resentful and distrustful when he thought of other ministers making decisions: he didn't want to devolve responsibility. But in all this excitement in action, with pleasure straining all the time into anxiety, right at the centre, where the little man sat, a spider, with his eyes always darting, searching for the next main chance, what was there? It is like trying to imagine the nucleus of an atom: what one found at the centre was electrical turbulence in an empty space.

At his desk, Hughes's normal mood was that he couldn't make up his mind. It was not just that he gathered on to his desk more business than he could manage but that a man who had spent his life orating, wheeling and dealing, speaking to briefs, conceptualising, at the age of fifty-three wanted to play administrator as well as politician, and he was no good at it. He had no skill in managing business. In his union days he had been a grandstander who took over when things became exciting, but who could leave the day-to-day work to faithful allies. But now he wanted to do the day-to-day work as well. His liking for jumping from one obsession to the next could still work—if he could find someone to take over before he lost interest—but he was neither himself capable enough nor able to summon a staff big enough and good enough to systematically move off his desk all the papers that he insisted on piling on top of it. With Andrew Fisher, papers passed from IN tray to OUT tray, with decisions written on them. Hughes had a good eye for detail, but only when the detail was exciting enough to be sharpened into a polemical edge. Failing that, with his long, bony fingers, he just muddled the papers around. In this sense, in the day-to-day routines of keeping the show going by keeping the paper moving, or by inquiring into the work of other ministers (the defence department was a picturesque state of mess) almost any other politician who had even half a belief in the war would have made a better prime minister. (Perhaps a certain scepticism about war can be useful in a prime minister.) Hughes, the prophet of action, was, in private, much of the time, unable to act. Instead, he would crackle with anger, perhaps raging at a furtive, inner glimpse of his own impotence, which he would then project outwards, on to others, and blame them for it. Regularly, he would retreat into neurotic periods of illness. By his inability to simplify the complexity of events into something he could believe in, and act upon with an hour-to-hour rationality, he would burst with fury—or relax in sarcastic wit. Action for him seemed to be something he did in front of others. It had to make a memorable anecdote, a grand public drama. By lunging into some scarcely-considered commitment, he could create a theatrical part for himself then for a while, as the audience watched, he would know what to do. He would have created an interim reality in which, as long as it lasted, he knew how to behave.

It was as an orator that he could most confidently define himself. Once he was up on the spruiking box, or the balcony, or the stage, he knew who he was and what to do. And it was in this, his most talented field, that as wartime prime minister he was to fail most significantly. Up to his hero's return to Australia in 1916 it had not been so: preaching crusades against an enemy is not unusual among prime ministers who have the stomach for it (although some manage without). In these performances he had simply changed briefs: the talents he had used to glorify the Labor Party, in particular the talent for defining an enemy and the talent for dramatising action, were now being used to glorify war. It was the Hun who was to be hated now, rather than the trusts and combines (although German trusts and combines were to be hated twice over, in a convenient double billing) and it was the cause of loyalty to the empire that was to be dramatised, rather than the cause of reform. But as he moved into the disorders of 1916 and 1917, disorders, one might argue, of his doing, he was, by his tongue, to turn Australians not against the Germans but against each other and help to cause the war itself to be doubted. This was not the act of a prudent wartime prime minister.

His greatest failure as a wartime prime minister was his incompetence as a politician who could thread together, and hold together, a wide coalition of support. Politicians are not necessarily administrators, although they may help liberate the talents of administrators, and they must be able to look as if they know what administrators are doing. Sometimes, like Hughes, they are brilliant illusionists, artists who, by creating worlds of rhetoric, sustain old values or conjure up new potentials, but even in this others do some of the magic. Politicians must, above all, be *politicians*. Suffering the secret humiliations of office and the recognition of its limits of power, in the job of manipulating the possible they work in a fog of ignorance and conflict, always dependent on others; sometimes in a contest they may be on the weakest side; sometimes in an alliance they may be the weakest partners. From the time he started to play his great theatrical role of prime minister of Australia Hughes walked like a man who had forgotten that part of his power lay with the labour movement.

It was while he was waking up England that Hughes's personal power base in Sydney started to disintegrate. When he returned to Australia, this seemed to be a matter beneath his concern. Yet when that power base went, he would spend the rest of his life with no power base other than his own reputation; he was to become a personal adventurer.

Chapter 4

Billy Hughes, Rat

❦ When Hughes arrived back in Australia *The Worker* greeted him with the headline WELCOME HOME TO THE CAUSE OF ANTI-CONSCRIPTION, with a reminder that twelve months before he had said: 'In no circumstances would I agree to send men out of this country to fight against their will.' But this was merely a wistful plea from past certainties to a present in which a new battle order had already formed. The New South Wales union movement was in revolt against Holman, but even more significantly most of the union movement throughout Australia was preparing for a war against conscription.

Through an infatuated stubborness and an increasing scepticism about the worth of the labour movement, Holman had isolated himself, and Hughes. In his refusal to reform the legislative council Holman had walked over the edge of the Labor Party's margin of toleration: the legislative council had blockaded those parts of Labor's reform program that Holman himself had not already abandoned, yet Holman had refused to control the council by appointing more Labor members to it. For several years he promised the state conference he would, but each time he broke his word—for the capricious reason that he had promised a seat in the council to a non-Labor friend, Hugh D. McIntosh, a theatrical entrepreneur and newspaper owner, whose company he enjoyed and whose money he had borrowed; if he wasn't allowed to appoint McIntosh he refused to appoint anybody. After this and other affronts from Holman, including (another reminder of the 1890s split) his coolness to a strike at Broken Hill, a union bloc, the 'Industrial Section' had formed, the most disciplined faction New South Wales Labor had ever seen, and in 1916 it outmanouevred Holman and stacked the state conference, a privilege Holman had previously kept to himself. The men running the industrial section used their numbers to censure Holman for not taking action on the legislative council; they wanted to humiliate him into accepting their power. That may have been all most of them wanted, but it was a trial of strength that left no further reserves for compromise. Holman began walking out of the party, as in a dream: perhaps the dream he followed was the belief of McIntosh and his friends that Holman could form a new centre party out of rightwing Labor and radical Liberals.

Meanwhile, in the coming battle against conscription, to a background of repressive regulations, censorship, gaolings, army raids on the headquarters of protest groups, prohibitions of meetings, police seizures of printing presses and the breaking up of rallies by soldiers, a number of small protest organisations had already sewn their banners and printed their pamphlets. In Broken Hill the mining union had sponsored a 'volunteer army' to fight conscription 'by every means'. Some organisations attacked others as too 'revolutionary', others as too 'bourgeois', but there was now evident one of those great miracles of the left—a gathering of strength in which could be assembled on one platform at one protest rally almost all of the many voices that were usually raised against each other, but were now urging people in more-or-less the same direction.

In the trades union movement, where scarcely a union had not declared itself, the division was no longer on conscription, but on whether force should be met by force, by calling a general strike to smash conscription if it came. The Victorian and Queensland Labor Parties had already demanded their MPs sign pledges opposing conscription; in New South Wales MPs were saved from this only by a temporary deal between politicians and machine. Twelve days after Hughes returned from Europe, his own electorate council on the Sydney waterfront passed a resolution opposing conscription; a month later even the Sydney Wharf Labourers' Union, the foundation stone of his union power, was to do the same. Resolutions and rallies supporting conscription were coming from all Hughes's political opponents—the Liberal Party branches, the chambers of commerce, the employers' organisations, joined by the bishops, professors, judges, editors.

Hughes had come back to Australia already knowing that he wanted to introduce conscription but he walked softly. Over the four weeks in which he was deciding how he would go about it, he made loud speeches to patriotic audiences and said—nothing. He was searching among leaders of the labour movement for allies but apart from the now desperate New South Wales MPs and a few other scattered groups of refugees, he could find no support, at least in the eastern states—except that of his own audacity, and his belief that the patriotic audiences were the same as public opinion. The man who for more than twenty years had thrilled to the power of his voice, and whose anecdotes were rich in how he had talked down committees, councils and whole hallfulls of doubters, was entranced by the view of himself speaking over the heads of the labour movement to the people of Australia.

The device he would use was a referendum: he was now lobbying for enough support from the party, not for conscription itself—that was impossible—but support to put through parliament a bill to call a referendum. In caucus, after twenty hours of talking over four days, at 2.30 one morning he achieved a majority of two from those who were still at the meeting. Two seemed enough.

If a calculating sense of national interest had been all that was to determine things in 1916, a prudent prime minister might have been concerned principally with keeping up the appearances of Australia's commitment as economically as possible; in this, maintaining a shining mirage of national unity would have been cheaper than trying to increase the numbers of young men herded for the slaughter. But in expressions of Australia's imperial loyalty it seemed inescapable that both blood and rhetoric should flow in excess: military alliance was not a moderate matter of calculation, but an unquestionable and greedy religion. Hughes allowed himself to be deceived by the British about the number of reinforcements required: accepting estimates which had doubled the number needed to keep the Australian divisions going, he passed these figures on to the voters and magnified the distortion by understating the success of voluntary recruiting. The combination of his lionising in Britain and the encouraging sound of his own voice in the guild halls and banqueting rooms had turned his head. He later told a secretary that he was talked into conscription by the British authorities and by powerful pressures in Australia. Whatever the reason for his change of view, having made the decision, he committed himself to it with the zealous fixedness of a charging rhinoceros. He had a new brief; he had therefore become a new person. Not only did it not occur to him that he could lose the referendum; neither did it occur to him that if he won the referendum, and tried to enforce conscription, even if the majority had said 'yes', within the minority there might be violent resistance—that, as Henry Lawson had put it, *blood might stain the wattle*.

Having got his two-vote majority for calling a referendum Hughes then tried to talk the party and union machines into supporting a YES vote. In Melbourne for three hours he gave the Victorian executive arguments they might like to hear, including the suggestion that conscription did not matter really...it was merely a shadow play...the war would be over soon...not many men were needed...it was a device to satisfy the British...and it might help shake German morale. But these devious assurances did not find one supporter. The next night he tried the Melbourne Trades Hall Council and again failed. In Sydney he told a different story, a story of Realpolitik, all done with shrugs and gestures and suggestively incomplete sentences: White Australia was in danger from the Japanese, only a few days' steam from Australia. The whole course of evolution in the Pacific had catastrophically come to a head...there was an ambassador in London...he had said to Hughes...Hughes had put him off...He was defeated, 21 to 5. At the Labor Council he again failed to find support. In the middle of the month the New South Wales Executive expelled Hughes from the Labor Party.

Three days later, he began his campaign, with a manifesto issued to the nation and a great meeting of an audience of those who usually voted against him in Sydney Town Hall. This was followed by wildly enthusiastic receptions from his former enemies in some of the most famous halls in Australia, as for forty days he put on the most ambitious personal show he had yet attempted. He moved from one long train journey to the next, with a typewriter for drafts of his speeches and a fountain pen with which to write what he thought on government documents. At each stop he would be met by cheering crowds and bundles of official telegrams requiring attention. His interpretation of government was of a series of decisions minuted by him on pieces of paper in railway carriages (without reference to others) in the spare time left between preparing and delivering speeches and recovering from neurotic illnesses. Australia itself was directly imperilled as one of Germany's richest prospective prizes: *Germany had long coveted this grand and rich continent, more than 14 times as large as Germany, and if she won, she would certainly claim it as an important part of her spoils. For this reason, the ramparts of our native land were on the allied trenches in France. If Britain fell, in Australia there would not be warfare but massacre. We would be like sheep before the butcher.* And as the campaign proceeded towards what was seen as inevitable success there was evidence of immediate threat from the International Workers of the World (IWW) groups whose syndicalist literature praised the virtues of sabotage and the general strike, and whose influence, along with that of German agents and Irish rebels ('Sinn Feinners') was projected as driving on the treachery of the NO campaign. In the fortnight before polling day, twelve IWW men were charged with treason, for raising insurgency against King George by setting alight various Sydney buildings. Their prosecutor railed against how their *fiendish and premeditated acts of arson, fiendish in design and devilish in ingenuity, had taken place after Mr Hughes's great and memorable speech*. Just before polling day a newspaper placard warned: IWW ASSASSINS WANT YOU TO VOTE NO.

Against this, the NO campaign included a simple patriotic appeal to race prejudice: *The ruling powers would import servile and cheap colored labor if it became lawful to send white men out to be shot down, led like sheep to the slaughter to make a fat man's holiday. This lonely outpost of the white man's civilisation would be deprived of its scanty garrison and left open to the cheap Asiatics, reduced to the social and economic level of Paraguay or some other barbarian country*. When it was learned that several hundred Maltese immigrants were coming to Australia, although at their own expense and on their own initiative, the NO campaigners gave this as proof that Hughes and the 'fat men', wanting a flood of cheap coloured labour, could not wait even until after they had won the referendum. One of the most popular NO posters said: VOTE NO AND KEEP AUSTRALIA WHITE.

For polling day a manifesto urging Australians to vote YES was signed by thirteen of the fourteen heads of government and opposition leaders in State and national politics; only T.J. Ryan the Queensland Labor premier did not sign it. Of the whole structure of official power and prestige in Australia the Queensland premier stood almost alone as an anti-conscriptionist. Yet his side won.

A fortnight after the referendum was defeated the Labor caucus met. By then six of Hughes's ministers had resigned, three of them not because of the conscription issue itself, but because of a provocative spasm of Hughes's near the end of the campaign. Only four of his government were still in office.

Hughes had already decided to leave the party and govern with opposition support, but, as a spinner of heroic sagas, he knew that the split needed a formal ceremony that would provide a memorable incident showing what it was all about. To provide the final anecdote in his twenty-three years' association with the party, he came to the caucus meeting and presided over his own notice of dismissal. Fifteen MPs spoke, all briefly, and all with the solemnity of men fighting over a significant event to see who would give it exemplary meaning. There were two attempts at a compromise, but Hughes didn't want a compromise. A large enough group of anti-conscriptionists were ready to join with the conscriptionists to give Hughes a majority in the party (although the minority might then have walked out) but Hughes didn't want a majority. When his time came to speak, using his jaunty style, he made points designed to come in handy in his coming battle against former comrades. He said his attackers were not speaking for themselves, but on instruction from an outside organisation. He was establishing the argument he would use for years afterwards that he had been a good Labor man, but he would not accept dictation from a 'junta' outside the party. He now provided the climax of the anecdote: he picked up his papers, and said 'Let all who support me follow me'. To a derisive cheer, he walked out of the room followed by twenty-four of the sixty-five members of the party. (One changed his mind, and went back.)

***

One of the most important ritualistic functions now for the Labor Party was to bury the dead, and lay solemn curses on Hughes so that appropriate meanings could derive from his treachery. Hughes, the renegade-in-chief, *the tinpot dictator who menaced the democracy of the Commonwealth, the unscrupulous and double-dyed trickster who had entered the camp of the enemy, the great leader of the working class who had sold out the workers to the silvertails and the plutocrats, the pocket Kaiser who had inflicted a damnable Prussian regime in Australia, was a traitor to the class that had raised him from obscurity and helplessness to power and fame, a champion of militarism, a whooper for war adopting the standpoint and outlook of the traditional foes of the common people.*

However, just as Hughes had argued that the death of soldiers had purified the nation, his enemies now claimed that his apostasy had purified the Labor Party: *The sheep had now been parted from the goats, the gold from the dross. For the crisis had shown the working class of our glorious continent the apostates willing to change their ideals for a mess of pottage; it had displayed the lairs of the jackals who had burst forth in all their horrid nakedness. From the festering slime of slander, dishonesty, abuse, scurrility and treachery had burst something beautiful and pure. And now that Labor had been through the fires of treachery and tribulation, let the word go forth that henceforth the objective shined, a brilliant light, straight ahead towards the New System, where there would be, for the first time, economic freedom and justice for all.*

For a while Labor people could dream that with the defeat of conscription the people were now on the move and things would never be the same again. But obviously the NO majority was not a Labor majority—there were too many country voters who had voted NO simply because they opposed conscription of farm labour, and would vote Liberal at an election—and in any case the victory depended on less than 42,000 votes. Nevertheless, there was the democratic exhilaration of a win against the powers of the land. Dominating the NO campaign was the State's coercive apparatus legitimised, by Hughes's fountain pen, preventing 'disaffection' and 'action prejudicial to recruiting' and expressed in bannings, spyings, raids, arrests and other acts of legal intimidation; and the YES campaign was supported by all the main newspapers, the Protestant churches, the general ideological 'establishment', most of the sporting and women's bodies, all the employers' organisations, a great deal of money, the commander of the Australian forces on the western front and the British commander-in-chief. Apart from what was left of the labour movement's own leaders, the only public figure on the NO side was the Catholic Archbishop Mannix, of Melbourne. He had spoken with wit and sarcasm that equalled, or outdid Hughes, so that in what was most noted in Hughes as a public entertainer he was now matched. Mannix did not speak often during the campaign, but his acts of individual drama helped offset the organisational flimsiness of the NO campaign, of which much was illegal—many leaflets were printed and distributed without being submitted to the censor—and while Hughes entertained Liberal voters in the town halls, most of the anti-conscription rallies were, through shortage of funds, held in the open air. Single-handed, in his intervention Mannix had expressed the frustrations and suspicions and longings, of those who saw themselves as working class, and, if they chose, they could find in his moderate arguments hints of darker meaning. For each person who heard him many others had been heartened by knowing that one so eminent had spoken in their cause.

The NO campaign had been improvised at one of those moments in history when at least a minority of manual workers and their families could see themselves as a class separate from all others, deprived, proud, threatened. Even the racism of the NO rhetoric was part of the theme that the reason for wanting conscription was that *the Australian workers were more advanced, more militant and more united than anywhere else and had become an example to the world*. In seeking to defend one nation, Hughes had helped create two.

***

In France, as winter came, the soldiers descended into the misery of savage rain and biting cold, in a world of mud so thick that they could sink up to their waists and so wide that much of the time was spent in laying duckboards across it, so that men could move, and in building wooden revetments against it, so that trenches and dugouts did not simply collapse. For relief, when the men rested behind the lines, 2,000 of them in a day would soak together in brewery vats filled with hot water and come out pink and warm while in buildings wet with steam a couple of hundred laundresses washed the filth out of their clothes. After the fiascoes which had killed or mutilated so many of their comrades they had bitterly lost faith in the general staff. The snow came, and then the frosts. For a month the mud was frozen into stone.

In April, in bleak squalls, men lay on the snow-covered ground near a railway embankment, then ran through a rain of bullets into a storm of fire in which the men of one brigade, bombed out by the Germans who had trapped them, were then shelled by their own artillery as they tried to escape; the brigade of 3,000 men suffered 2,339 casualties. This was an opening blow near the village of Bullecourt, in what the new French commander saw as the decisive and final campaign of the war. A month later, as the houses of Bullecourt were pounded into rubbish, through clouds of dust the Australians were again sent out to die. Over the fields they went towards the Hindenburg Line, capturing a section of its concrete strengthened walls and concrete dugouts and holding it through seven major German counter attacks, and a dozen or so minor ones, a small allied foothold deep in German territory, constantly bombed and shelled. The French commander's plan failed so speedily and obviously that he was dismissed; for some weeks many of the French troops mutinied. Bullecourt cost the Australians 10,000 casualties.

A month later masked Australians stumbled in the dark

through woods stagnant with German phosgene gas and then lined up at the white tapes marking the jumping-off point for the advance on Messines ridge in Flanders, where the British commander was now carrying out *his* plan: the whole countryside shook as nineteen great bubbles of earth ballooned up and then burst into flames that coloured the dark clouds red. Through the dust of smoke and debris left by the explosion of these nineteen huge mines, the largest explosions yet known in wartime, the Australians advanced over the shattered earth into a new fear—concrete pillboxes where machine gun bullets sprayed at them until the Australians could butcher the men within, sometimes in their fear killing all, including the wounded and those who were trying to surrender. Despite this new terror, Messines ridge was seized.

For the first time the Australians had taken part in a British offensive that was successful; there had been careful preparation beforehand—seven days' bombardment, thirty-six successive memoranda outlining tactics, a large model of the battlefield to study—and now there was training for the rationality of the new 'step by step' technique in which in the opening stages a ballet movement of artillery shells advanced slowly and carefully in front of the soldiers; then, to give the soldiers time to bomb the pillboxes and dig trenches a light protective barrage would play in front of them, while a roaming barrage ruffled the enemy; after half an hour the main barrage would come back to the soldiers again and dance them on for another 500 metres, then split into protective and roaming barrages until massing together again after an hour or so, to lead the soldiers on once more.

When the soldiers went back into a major battle, near Ypres, at dawn on 20 September, through smoke and mist, this new technique worked almost exactly to time table. Six days later, through smoke and dust, it worked again. Eight days later another advance (through smoke and steam, after light rain) went as it was meant to. Then the weather broke: guns were bogged; ambulances capsized;

the rain increased from showers and squalls to a thick torrent. On 9 October, in an attempted attack on Passchaendale village, rationality dissolved in the mud; the soldiers went out, then fell back onto the white tapes from which they had started, leaving their dead and wounded behind. In one of the war's most memorably dreadful struggles, the soldiers had returned to their familiar state of murderous fiasco. Now it was seen that what had seemed a grand strategy, was nothing more than individual acts of rationality in the black madness of the British commander's mind. The very shells whose fall, in their ballet of death, had seemed so reasonably planned had blown up the drainage system in a valley of reclaimed marsh: with the rain, the valley turned into a swamp. At the end of the four-month disaster of the Ypres offensive, which cost the British 400,000 men, one of the staff officers who had planned it drove up and looked at the area he had disposed of so cleverly on the map. 'My God', he said, in tears, 'did we really send men to fight in that?'

In Australia, posters of the Huns in their spiked helmets threatened immediate disaster to passengers in trams and trains and ferries, to window-shoppers and hotel-drinkers.

In one poster the Hun was a gorilla in a spiked helmet, his hairy arms drenched in blood; in another a firing party of Huns had penetrated an Australian's backyard and were about to execute him in front of his own corrugated-iron water tank, while flames burned in the background and his womenfolk screamed. Some of the appeals were more gentle than this: *A Free Trip to Europe!...Take Up the Sword of Justice!...Quick! We Want Men! Do It Now!...Don't read history—Make it!...To Arms! Play the Game! Looking On Is Not Cricket!...The Anzacs Are Cooeeing!...Would You Scab On An Anzac?* But it was the Hun, assassin of Edith Cavell and organiser of corpse factories where human bodies were boiled down to make soap, who was the greatest threat to humankind the world had ever known.

As well as the Hun himself there were others to hate on

'the home front'...shirkers in unions...disloyal and rebellious Sinn Feiners like Mannix...sinister war profiteers...and men who were too yellow to enlist. The white feather became the primary instrument of exorcism for those who wanted to drive out the yellow streak. The 'returned soldiers' were becoming one of the angry voices in the street. At open-air meetings they might break up labour platforms; in retaliation, unionists might break up meetings of 'returned men.'

In the labour movement the war was now being seen by some as a bosses' war, a trade war, a capitalist's bloodbath, but most who saw the war this way would not speak of it loudly, for fear of arrest. For other (probably most) workers the war remained, in balance, something that had to be fought, and they were proud of the fighting men, finding in them symbols of Australian working-class traditions of boldness and comradeship but they saw Mr Fat using the war to make excessive profits and to smash the unions and workers' wages and conditions. For them, the 'shirkers' were not the men with yellow streaks but the rich, with golden linings in their pockets from the war, but paying little of their own money towards its costs.

In the homes of those Australians who had enlisted, the war was a matter for pride and fear. In tens of thousands of homes a modest domestic shrine had been erected—a framed photograph of a son or a husband or a father in uniform, placed in a special spot and decorated with regimental colours—there was a shared pride in how the 'Aussies', (as the Australian soldiers were now being called) despite the bungles of the British 'brass', were performing so bravely 'on the other side', but there was fear if a telegraph messenger came into a street: he might be bringing the message of a brave boy's wounding. There was special fear in an unexpected doorknock: it might be a clergyman, bringing news of a brave boy's death.

After three years, seventeen million men were already dead or wounded. The frontline troops of the countries fighting the war saw themselves as history's unique victims.

In most countries there were food shortages and in each country inflation brought distress to the poor, reduced the value of the savings of 'the little people' and created distrust, and hatred. The 'war profiteers', the 'sharks', the 'merchants of death' could be hated as much as the enemy. In each country propaganda degraded with its lies and there were new depravities in the name of nation, race and empire. In each country, if in small groups, there was again talk of revolution and some disgust with socialist collaboration with militarist governments. Despite the war, in 1917 in each country there were strikes; in imperial Russia strikes and then riots, turned protectors into revolutionaries and introduced a new era in history.

***

Behind the disorders of the western front were the incessant rivalries between generals, between politicians, between politicians and generals, and between national governments. Competing ambitions of political and military leaders decided men's deaths: despite the tumult and the slaughter of the war there was the continuing scramble for its glittering prizes. Among those who struggled to maintain power, and used policy for this purpose, was W. M. Hughes. Whatever other motives prompted him to offend the labour movement so carelessly in 1915, and to divide both the labour movement and the nation so neatly in 1916, one can assume that he had not forgotten he was prime minister of a government due to fight an election in 1917 and that he wanted to win. From the time he was sworn in on 14 November 1916, as leader of the 'National Labor' government, a government based on the smallest party in parliament, his principal concern must have been simply to survive.

To understand how he survived it is useful to know how he played bridge. When he learned the game, he played it in a manner different from everyone else. His main aim was not to win, but to dominate the game. He did all the talking and joking and laughing and complaining; he also tried to do all the bidding...Down two tricks...down three tricks...down four tricks...going down made no difference to Hughes. Winning tricks was not what he was principally after. What he really wanted was to overbid everyone else, keep all the initiatives and play every hand. It was by similar methods from 1916 to 1922 that he kept his position as prime minister of Australia.

He was uniquely detested by old colleagues and constantly distrusted by new. He was soon to have no friends in his own government. For the next six years there were always some colleagues pressing to restrain his adventurings; usually some were plotting to get rid of him. He necessarily devoted much of his time to private finagling, playing off one against the other, blocking rivals, building shifting coalitions of support, but his main play was to impress his rivals with what could look like a unique command over public opinion. To do this, as in bridge, he had to keep all the initiatives and command all the public attention. He was the one who had to do all the talking and do all the bidding. The tale spinner of 'Oleander Lodge' had now become an epic bard for a part of the nation.

During the rest of the war he had to maintain the illusion of himself as its supreme upholder so that enemies among his collaborators might be afraid to pull him down in front of their own supporters. His view of himself demanded high winds of continuous public turmoil to sustain his personality, but in wartime the turmoil he threw up could meet an answering public need. Many people wanted the war to be accompanied by loud and fearsome shouts; Hughes seemed the loudest and most fearsome shouter. More noisily than anyone else, he could sound as if he wanted to win the war. And he could define the war as many people wanted it defined: for them, he gave it the right meaning. For others, the endearing touches of impishness that came from his gnome-like bravado and his dwarf's wit could add to his style the spice of a David challenging a Goliath. He could seem a little man fighting the little man's big battles. There was a priceless consolation for those conservatives who thought it more seemly that big battles should be fought by a big man: the very talents for sowing division that made Hughes such a destructive national leader were useful in mutilating the labour movement.

From 1916 to 1922, usually exhausted, often sick, he was a gambler, sometimes in a sudden move enjoying quick spurts of success, but often living in terror of being caught out. Always ahead of him, in his vision, would be the gleaming emblems of some victory only he was worthy enough to gain; but he would live mostly among dark perils and anxieties, enlivened by boastful merry tales of deceit and tricks. He would live in a tormented and lonely private world of tantrums, muddles, distrust and often fear: then, as, to the cheering crowd, he made yet another speech, he would inflate himself to life size by his own breath.

Come back to him now, at the end of November 1916, when parliament resumed its sittings. It is a month after his defeat in the referendum and a fortnight after the last rites have been performed over his abandonment of the Labor Party. He is prime minister of a government whose party controls only fourteen votes out of seventy-five in the house of representatives and only eleven out of thirty-six in the senate. In the house of representatives he relies for a majority on the support of his old enemies, the Liberal Party; the senate is controlled by his new enemy, the Labor Party, now renamed 'Australian Labor Party' to distinguish it from Hughes's 'National Labor Party'.

Already, in Collins Street, Melbourne, in what had been the headquarters rooms of the YES campaigners, some of the most conservative of the Liberals are conferring with some of the most political of the businessmen to launch a new 'Win the War' party. To begin with, Hughes won't have anything to do with it, then, in one of those sudden jumps that are his nature (probably, in this case, because he now sees he has nowhere else to go) he gatecrashes the new movement and puts himself at its head. It is he who signs the circulars whose language had already been drafted in Collins Street and he who chairs the meeting in the town hall to launch the 'National Federation' with Collins Street rhetoric. But now the Liberals see his weakness: if he needs them, do they need him? Cook denounces the National Federation; Holman, now leader in New South Wales of a fusion of conscriptionist Labor MPs with the Liberals, denounces Hughes as a spent force. Some of the Liberals want to see Hughes thrown out of politics because his public style of sarcasm and hatred has bred a sense of division in the nation; others see him as still a socialist; at least three of the Liberals want him out because each of them wants his job. It is only when Cook, who is one of these, decides that keeping a rival Liberal out of the prime ministership is more important than defeating Hughes, that he starts to deal with Hughes. Three months after its birth, Hughes's 'National Labor Party' dies in the embrace of the Liberal Party, to produce the 'National Party.'

There is some uncertainty about the name. Is it the National Party? The Nationalist Party? The Win the War Party? There is no uncertainty about its nature. It is the old Liberal Party with a new name, with a somewhat wider branch membership and some Labor Party defectors for decoration. Hughes is now locked into the main conservative political structures in Australia.

In the patriotic task of maintaining himself as prime minister, his next move is to try to avoid an election by extending the life of parliament. Standing in his way is the Labor majority in the Senate; but this majority disappears when three Tasmanian Labor Party senators are persuaded to look more carefully to their health. One resigns, giving health reasons. One retires to hospital. One, for health reasons, goes on a long sea voyage. There follow allegations that Hughes has tried to bribe another Labor senator. In Tasmania the Hobart *Mercury* speaks of Hughes as a 'talented conjuror' and a 'trickster' and with that local idiosyncracy that can mark Tasmanians, and also with some of that distaste that individual conservatives are to go on showing for Hughes's trickiness, two Tasmanian Nationalist senators withdraw support. Hughes calls an election.

Three days before he is to open his campaign in Bendigo Town Hall (he has retreated to Bendigo from the Sydney waterfront, where there is no hope that the workers would vote for him) Holman's Nationalist Party in New South Wales wins a twenty-seat majority. Hughes's election seems safe enough now. But to make sure of it, he pledges that there will be no conscription without another referendum, and then only if national safety demands it.

Hughes won the election with nearly 55% of the vote. That got him through until May. Then an eruption in the labour movement temporarily diverted his enemies in his own party—the 'great strike' of August-September 1917, one of the most impressive dramas, and one of the most sharply remembered, in the labour movement's history. In the May election the Labor vote had dropped from 51% to 44%, a heart-rending result for Labor supporters, the worst since 1906, when the party was still establishing itself, made all the worse because, only a year before, the Labor Party could still seem as if it were becoming the natural and permanent governing party in Australia. What was there for them now? In the kind of spirit that can drive workers to desperate ambitions, the workmen themselves began to develop some of that feeling towards a *general strike* that, for years, the red raggers had talked about, although now seventy of the red raggers, the remnants of the IWW, were about to go to gaol. When an attempt at a trial of strength came from the railway commissioners in New South Wales, the railwaymen expressed their disgust with life by coming out—mostly ahead of decisions from their unions. Pit by pit, the miners closed down the coal mines, although with plenty of coal at grass they were equally weak; the Broken Hill metal ore miners came out; wharf labourers stopped work; the coal lumpers and seamen joined them. Others came out...gas workers, slaughtermen, tramwaymen, warehousemen, electrical tradesmen, workers in the sugar and liquor trades, sacrificing themselves to their disillusion. Mainly by rank-and-file decisions, often with leaders trying to control them, workmen were expressing their unhappiness in the only effective democratic method available to them. The strikers were denounced as *the tools of anarchists, revolutionaries, German agents and political desperadoes out for mob rule and deliberately attempting rebellion against the orderly government of the community*. In the name of law and discipline, the New South Wales government ordered police arrests of three leaders of the strike defence committee; they were arrested at midnight; documents and money were seized from the Labor Council. The government commandeered lorries, carts, motor vehicles, colliers; it doubled the police force, established volunteer camps for the male strikebreakers and set up Women's Loyal Service Bureaus for the females. For their part, the strikers organised daily processions, singing 'Solidarity Forever' as they marched through the city with banners and bands to the Domain. There were 40,000 of them in one march; at one Sunday meeting 100,000 people listened to union orators preach that apocalypse that had also been preached in the 1890s in the Domain when Hughes did his spruiking. They were told that *in their fight against tyranny the workers had taken the field, and swept into battle in the greatest fight for liberty Australia had ever known.*

For a short season the strikers could imagine what victory might have been like—something that many would never again be able to imagine. When the strike was smashed, unions were deregistered, tame unions set up, workers blacklisted, preference for jobs given to free labour. What was being checked was not just the strike, but the gains unionism had made since the 1890s.

The strike had given Hughes another couple of months' respite from those who wanted to get rid of him. It had been essential for him to pull the fiercest possible faces in his whole wardrobe of masks. Previously he had intervened in strikes with a strength and diplomacy intended to end them, not to provoke the strikers into catastrophe; even after the Labor split he had intervened in a big coalfields' strike by setting up a superficially 'impartial' special commissioner, and then bluntly instructing him to meet the men's claims (thereby giving the miners their best strike settlement for thirty years). Now it was essential for his political future to make a lot of noise about being not a solver of industrial disputes, but a breaker of strikes. He acted out this part with that zeal necessary for him to add to any cause: he set up a National Service Bureau to recruit volunteer labour, gave himself power to commandeer coal stocks and, when pressure was being put on the Australian Workers' Union (AWU) to join the strike, (a move that might have transformed the struggle) he gave himself power to deregister the AWU. When, in the punitive victories that followed the strike, the Commonwealth arbitration court disappointed the union-smashers by refusing to deregister the Waterside Workers' Federation, Hughes pelted the court with abuse. A year before he had still been president of the federation.

The candidate of those who wanted to get rid of Hughes was now William Irvine, a politician knight and former Victorian premier, one of the initiators of the 'Win the War Party', and a man to whom the belief in conscription had become the gravest matter in human existence. Hughes had retired, exhausted and ill, to Port Macquarie on the New South Wales north coast, where he had been ordered to take a month's rest. After he had settled in, he heard that Irvine (who had criticised Hughes's promise not to introduce conscription without another referendum) had launched a conscription campaign in the eastern states.

Because Hughes had turned recruiting into a bitterly divisive political matter, the number of recruits had run down; with strong press support, Irvine was now playing on feelings that the Aussies on the western front were being stabbed in the back by shirkers back home. With a great deal of business money behind it, Irvine's campaign proceeded with a full show of public meetings, inspirational banners, brass bands and the clashing cymbals of newspaper editorials. Then, after two weeks' rest, Hughes heard something that sent him at once to spend a weekend in Sydney: some of Irvine's supporters had been stupid enough to approach Hughes's secretary to see if, for a large salary, he would help organise an anti-Hughes campaign. Over the weekend in Sydney Hughes talked to Cook—who, if he was not himself to replace Hughes was determined that no one else would—and they decided to outflank Irvine by calling another conscription referendum, which they did simply by issuing a regulation. Hughes has a good story at hand: the Italian army had collapsed at Caporetto... national safety was in danger. To maintain his power it seemed to Hughes that he needed a referendum. So he called one.

Off he went again, on the fourth great war of words he had fought since becoming prime minister. First, the Wake Up England campaign, then the conscription referendum, then the election; now another referendum. For most of November and December, with the business of government following him in combinations of short and long electrical impulses passing over the telegraph wires, in the summer heat he travelled thousands more kilometres, back through the familiar railway stations and town halls. This time, because he was getting threatening letters, he carried a gun in his hip pocket, but the words he fought with were mostly the same: he was still combating *the systematic campaign of poisonous doctrine insidiously disseminated throughout the country* by last year's enemies—the German agents and the Sinn Feiners. What was new was that the men *responsible for the great strike which had paralysed our industries, the kind of men who today were in power in Russia* were now added to those who *were playing the game of Germany*. It was also new that Australia's national safety was imperilled by happenings in Italy. Another significant development was the participation of the Returned Soldiers and Sailors Imperial League of Australia, with a manifesto that, in an early example of lest-we-forget language, began: *Rouse ye then, ye Anzacs, put forth all your strength, your energy and your eloquence. Organise and carry the flag to fight the Hunnish foe throughout the length and breadth of this great Commonwealth.*

With his talent for arousing accusations of 'petty juggling and trickery', Hughes said that, although the last conscription campaign had demanded 16,500 recruits each month to maintain the Australian divisions, now only 7,000 were needed. He aroused further distrust when he announced that free speech would prevail, then tightened censorship. The new censorship stirred up hatred amongst members of his own party in New South Wales where the censors deleted from NO propaganda 'gross falsehoods' about Hughes but left in 'gross falsehoods' about Holman; and in Queensland, it enabled Premier Ryan to cleverly turn Hughes into an absurd figure of frustrated malice. In a smart Queensland trick, after the censor had deleted parts of speeches by Ryan and others, the censored politicians read their censored speeches into Hansard so that they could be legally printed and distributed; Hughes had the military authorities raid the government printer and seize the Hansards. When Ryan repeated his censored statements outside parliament, Hughes had him prosecuted. But Hughes lost the case. Ryan was already being seen, as Hughes was in his day, as the most talented man in the Labor Party, and Hughes had now turned him into a national figure who could outsmart Hughes. And Mannix was drawing them in—his great showmanship and his powers of wit, ridicule and invective could attract crowds of up to 100,000, come to cheer a great prophet and laugh with a great clown. When Ryan spoke in the Sydney Domain he brought a crowd reckoned at 120,000.

Speakers were regularly shouted down and meetings broken up; eggs, bottles and road metal were thrown and the police sometimes drew their batons. Among these reports of disorder a meeting Hughes addressed at a Queensland country railway station provided what for several decades remained one of the best remembered anecdotes about him. The anecdote had many versions. In the most extreme (improvised by Hughes and some of the newspapers on the day) Hughes was in great danger. Desperadoes armed with spanners and hammers stood threateningly; he was assaulted in a sudden tumult by a number of men in what virtually amounted to a riot. From this he emerged, gallantly dishevelled, his knuckles bleeding. In the least extreme version (and also, perhaps the truth) an egg hit his hat and when he ran from the platform a sergeant in plain clothes caught hold of him and tried to quieten him down; the men 'armed with hammers and spanners' were a train examiner with his wheel-tapping hammer and a railway workman with a spanner, both on their normal job. In all versions of the anecdote Hughes ordered the sergeant to arrest two men and the sergeant refused, so, after a public squabble with Ryan, who supported the sergeant, Hughes founded the Commonwealth Police.

This time the referendum was lost by 94,000 votes. Newspapers and enemies in his own party blamed Hughes: he should never have made the pledge not to introduce conscription without a referendum—this was no time for democracy, but for action, and conscription should have been introduced without reference to the people. Alternatively Hughes was attacked as undemocratic and his intemperate oratorical pursuit of political enemies was seen as turning people against both voluntary recruiting and conscription, even against the war itself. In New South Wales, first the attorney-general and then Holman presented Hughes as *a man who had failed in the hour of crisis; he had broken his word continuously and systematically under the pressure of hysteria; his guarantees were as valueless as a German treaty; his erratic tendencies were a source of danger to Australia. The members of the National Party in the Federal*

Parliament should choose another leader—one whose judgement could be trusted and on whose promises people might rely, rather than one who had never been loyal to anybody or to anything.

As Hughes spent Christmas at the small farm he had bought at Sassafras, a hill resort near Melbourne, while in Sydney Holman and his attorney-general were calling for his dismissal, the special predicament he had to wriggle out of was that he had left himself open to his enemies in the party because in his opening thunder in the Bendigo Town Hall at the beginning of the referendum campaign he had said: 'I tell you plainly that the government must have this power. It cannot govern the country with it and will not attempt to do so.' It was a last-minute decision, made in the train on the way to Bendigo, another of the last throws of a gambler who had enjoyed many a successful last throw. Now, as a gambler who knew how not to pay his debts, he had to demonstrate that he *could* govern the country without conscription.

The first step was to have the parliamentary party behind him. On 3 January the party began a two-day meeting. On the first day Hughes pulled a bold face, spoke solemnly of the best interests of the country and of the empire, and after five hours got a confidence vote of sixty-three to two. Overnight some of the malcontents gave each other enough courage to have another go: when the meeting resumed on the next day and they moved that Hughes be replaced by a candidate of their own the number ready to vote against him went from two to seven. There were more than this who wanted to get rid of Hughes, but they weren't yet ready to put up their hands and say so. For the moment Hughes could still look as if he had the party behind him. Now, so that he could look as if he cared about his pledge at Bendigo, Hughes formally resigned to the governor-general and, one after the other, seven taxis dropped political leaders at government house while the governor-general 'sought advice'. The seventh visitor, the treasurer, Sir John Forrest, was bold enough to give the advice that he, Forrest, should replace Hughes. Forrest spent two hours putting his case: Hughes was too autocratic...he was a muddler and a meddler...his real concerns were not with the business of government, but 'limelight exhibitions'. The governor-general was sympathetic: he thought that by staying in office Hughes was losing face. Taxis then brought back to government house two of the National Party leaders who had already been there. They stuck by Hughes. After dinner Hughes was told that he was again prime minister. As a reward for disloyalty, Hughes quickly caused Forrest to be made a peer—'Lord Forrest of Bunbury' was the first Australian elevated to the house of lords—then took a gnome's delight in telling Forrest that one so elevated now had to resign from Australian politics. His dishing of Forrest became another memorable Billy Hughes anecdote, unmarred by the fact that Forrest was dying of cancer.

To understand the turbulent uncertainty in which Hughes continued to live, imagine the next few weeks. When parliament meets, the Labor members try to exploit Hughes's breaking of yet another pledge. At the same time, rebels in Hughes's own party patch together alliances and put on shows of strength intended to overcome the caution of politicians who will not commit themselves until they know who will win; one of these is a comforting scheme that a minority Liberal group might govern with the support of the Labor Party. Fourteen Nationalists are ready to vote against Hughes in the house.

The next month the director-general of recruiting circulates a secret report that, in effect, without saying so directly, blames Hughes's political methods for the discord and distrust that have damaged voluntary recruiting. A go-between with government house offers the governor-general the idea of calling a conference of all the parties, to take the politics out of recruiting. Like all the governors and governors-general, Munro-Ferguson sees his job as that of a loyal British agent. (His official secretary, as representative in Australia of the British secret service had set up a small Australian secret service which, for a while, he ran from government house.) He therefore likes the idea of creating a new concord that will serve the interests of his own country. He puts the idea forward as his own and sounds out the Labor leaders, who agree to a conference, and Hughes, who doesn't agree—perhaps because co-operation between the Labor Party and the Nationalists on recruiting might lead to co-operation on other matters; his position may depend on the continuance of discord.

The battle on the western front makes Hughes change his mind. On 21 March 1918, after a surprise two-hours' barrage from 4,000 guns, shock troops moved swiftly through the gas and mists and passed across sixty kilometres of a front line where the defenders' communications had been blown up; two days later they were capturing depots well behind the front. The defenders ordered a general retreat and within a week the victors advanced nearly sixty kilometres. The breakthrough that had been talked about so often now seemed to have come about. But it was a German breakthrough. In a crisis of this kind, one which Hughes can employ to his advantage, he now agrees to the governor-general's conference, and on the first day of a two-day meeting of the Nationalists' caucus, he tells his party about this decision as part of his general message that party solidarity is essential at a time of such grave international crisis. Sick with influenza, he is again in one of his stages of near breakdown. Unmoved, the rebels attack Hughes's failure to take more advantage of the party's 'best business brains' but when parliament resumes on 5 April he plays another strong card: he moves a motion applauding the heroic efforts of the allied and Australian troops and affirming Australia's determination to fight on to secure a victorious peace and the freedom of the world. Outside parliament house, 1,500 supporters of Mannix are singing 'God Save Ireland' and songs satirising Hughes, and two days previously the Victorian State Labor Conference had passed a resolution using disloyal phrases such as 'discussion of peace' and 'peace terms', so it is no surprise to Hughes when in the house of representatives, Labor backbenchers fall into his trap. While, in the senate, Labor gives quick unanimous support to the motion, and joins in the singing of 'God Save the King', in the house of representatives Labor men attack the motion. They use the disloyal phrase 'peace by negotiation' and argue that peace should be 'equitable' or 'honourable' rather than 'victorious'. Six hours of this remind Nationalists thinking of supporting the Nationalist rebels of the infamy of Labor, 'with its friends in Russia'. On the same day it is announced that Irvine has become chief justice of Victoria. Another one out of the way.

On 10 April 40,000 people meet in and near the Exhibition Building in Melbourne to affirm their devotion to the Crown and display by their actions their disapproval of the disloyalty of a recent Catholic rally. The next day Hughes is too sick to attend parliament; his speech giving the government's plans is read out for him and is seen by the newspapers as disappointing. On the following day, his government is attacked in parliament by members of his own party. The next day, the attacks continue...*the administration is extravagant and faulty...it is time there was someone who understood business methods*. On the following day, when the governor-general opens the all-party conference, with its *bold call to end all strife,* Hughes isn't there: as a political device, he has created a parliamentary crisis by treating the Nationalist attacks on his government as a motion of no confidence and the rebels are privately being threatened that if they try to vote Hughes out, he will call a general election. On the next day the newspapers print the order-of-the-day of Haig, the British commander: *There is no other course open to us but to fight it out. Every position must be held till the last man. With our backs to the wall and believing in the justice of our cause, each of us must fight to the end.*

On the same day, with his own back to the wall, Hughes makes his first appearance at the governor-general's conference and launches a prepared offensive into Labor territory. Now that Hughes is there, men become angry; when he attempts to read from what he says is a cable from London showing how serious the German breakthrough has become, they shout him down and one Labor man, sceptical of any document produced as part of this orator's gestures, calls out: 'We've had enough of your forgeries'. Hughes picks up his deaf aid and bursts out of the room into the military secretary's office and tells the military secretary to take away himself and his typist and all of the papers. Associates join Hughes. They set up a war council. They return to the angry and useless debate.

Still plagued by influenza, three days later Hughes goes back to parliament, makes a speech in what he has dramatised as a no-confidence debate, then calls five of the rebels into his room and asks for their loyalty. He has tried to bluff them into declaring confidence. They refuse, and at three o'clock the next morning when the division comes they join Labor in voting against confidence in the government. But Hughes still has a majority. The next day, 19 April, the governor-general's all-party conference ends in fiasco.

Several days later Hughes, having made some party political points in his patriotic speech at the Anzac Day luncheon at the Millions Club, is out on the Pacific Ocean in the SS *Niagara,* with his solicitor-general, his secretary and his personal physician, his new press officer, his wife and their daughter Helen, now in her third year and still object of his special affection. With him are Cook and John Latham, Cook's adviser. In the afternoon Hughes plays deck quoits, at which he encourages his opponents to let him win. At night they travel with lights out and all port holes closed. They do not know it, but events are going to keep them away from Australia for sixteen months. By then 60,000 Australian soldiers will have died, the highest casualty rate of any empire army. The empire will have won the war. And Hughes will have become a legend, as the Little Digger.

Chapter 5

The Little Digger

✧ The central ceremonial axis in the Australian national capital is the three kilometres, some of it a processional way, some of it lake, some of it gardens, that connect parliament house with the Australian War Memorial. It is not parliament house but the byzantine confidence of the war memorial—in appearance both mosque and fort—that dominates this axis, as if the principal assertion to be made about Australians is that they are warriors.

At the time the memorial was planned, a great many Australians would have seen such an assertion as the truth. *That the war was the pivotal event in the history of Australia is beyond dispute,* said Ernest Scott, the official historian of the home front. The war was the means by which Australians, having provided *one of the most notable fighting forces in history, had secured a recognised place among the nations,* said C. E. W. Bean, as historian of the war itself the highest guardian of this legend. *Tested by the fire of courage and self sacrifice,* Australians had proved so true that they had now indisputably come of age.

Within the memorial in the courtyard, there are a Commemorative Stone and a Pool of Reflection; in the cloisters the bronze panels of the roll of honour list the dead; in the Hall of Memory stained glass windows, mosaics and bronze sculpture commemorate the *resource, candour, devotion, curiosity, independence, comradeship, ancestry, patriotism, chivalry, loyalty, coolness, control, audacity, endurance* and *decision* of those in the army, navy, air force and women's services who, *when extinction threatened, remained resolute in the cause of country, freedom and humanity.* The tourists spend most of their time in the galleries looking at the display of the robes and vestments of the Great War, its holy relics (Turkish horse shoes, the furthermost Australian water bottle found at Gallipoli, a typewriter, a trumpet, a lieutenant-colonel's boots *bearing the sacred soil of Anzac,* a brigadier-general's tin mug, bibles, wire cutters, shovels, a whistle...), its way stations (dioramas of the attack on Lone Pine, of the battle of Romani, of the evacuation of the wounded on the Western Front...) and its icons *(The Landing at Gallipoli, Zero Hour at Messines, The Battle of Beersheba...)*

Throughout Australia, fashioned in granite, bronze, sandstone, marble and stained glass, are thousands of monuments to the nationhood achieved by sacrifice in war. In Melbourne there is a shrine in the manner of the mausoleum of a prince of ancient Persia, in Sydney a sanctuary in 1930s Aztec, in Brisbane a sacred circle of doric columns, in Adelaide a granite arch, in Perth a granite pylon, in Hobart a granite obelisk, in Ballarat an arch of victory and an avenue of honour, in Newcastle a cultural centre, in Geelong a memorial hall, in Bathurst a carillon, in Bendigo a replica of the London cenotaph; on a hill in Albury a floodlit column, on a hill in Goulburn a floodlit tower, on Mount Macedon near Melbourne a floodlit cross. There are memorial schools, memorial plaques, memorial drinking fountains, memorial bas reliefs, memorial groves, memorial foyers, memorial cairns; in church after church there are warriors chapels with flames of remembrance; and, in every town or suburb, a column or a statue, or an obelisk was set up as a wayside shrine not only to the fallen, but to the new cult of a nationhood earned in blood.

As well as heroes in bronze or marble or stained glass there were also living heroes, the 'Returned Men'. Round bronze badges were given to them, to honour their achievement, and for those incapacitated by suffering there was a special silvery badge. In a tram or a pub, walking down the street, going to the pictures, one could see at a glance who had served the nation and who had not.

'Anzac' was so sacred that it became a protected word—the British as well as the Australian parliament prohibited its use for any purpose except those authorised by the government—and Anzac Day became the national day, with the privilege of proclaiming national values.

The two values chosen were nation-creating and empire loyalty. In celebrating nation-creating, Anzac Day reminded Australians that *Australia was young in the company of nations but its nationhood had been earned in the glorious epic of Anzac bravery, which had given the word Australia meaning. The history of Australia had begun with a blank space on the map and ended with the record of a new name on the map, that of Anzac.* In celebrating the empire, it reminded Australians that *under the Union Jack all men were free and that was why so many had died to keep the flag flying high. Through discipline and self sacrifice the Anzacs had followed the magnetism of kinship and shown unswerving loyalty and devotion to the sacred duties of empire.*

But something was to be added to these two sets of values. The Returned Men won out over those myth-makers who wanted the soldiers to bear only the Roman virtues of rural simplicity, stoic self-discipline and self sacrifice, as described by Cicero and Seneca and translated into school text books. Beginning with the Anzacs themselves on Gallipoli, the soldiers forced something of their own homely presence into the legend of nation-creators and empire-sustainers. Now they took the right to be represented at their own funeral: the rituals of Anzac Day were to include not only processions and assemblies, but glorifications of gambling, drunkenness and general comradeship and good fellowship. To the dogmas of nation and empire that came from platform and pulpit had been added a sense of a folk democracy and some touches of a people's scepticism: the Returned Men had taken as their national legacy the magical attributes of *mateship* which had democratic qualities (among others) and even if masters of ceremonies found it embarrassing, some of the rhetoric of mateship had to be added to the rhetoric of empire and nation; on 25 April, Australians were also to be reminded that *Anzac Day was a solemn sacrament of mateship. A more thoroughly democratic army had never before fought, but however impatient they were of saluting and ceremonial, they could do the right thing and never let down a mate.*

In their folk idealisation of themselves, the soldiers found a new word. They went beyond the idea of 'the Anzac' (most had not been at Gallipoli) and 'the Aussie' (which passed on to sporting teams and Australians generally); they created instead the folk idea of 'the Digger', a usage perhaps first developed by New Zealand soldiers, but something Australians had taken to themselves by the middle of 1917. We do not know whether the word, based on the digging essential in trench warfare, was a revival of the old goldfields' term for a miner, or referred to both, but just as 'mate', first used in the 1840s and then on the goldfields with a strictly defined meaning similar to that of the United States 'pardner', had been broadened to cover the general ideas of comradeship, 'digger' was first used in a restricted manner—an alternative for 'cobber' in the second person form of address—and was then broadened to suggest the special quality of Australian soldiers, and then of the Returned Men. They were 'the Diggers'.

In the mysteries of folk creation, in which new habits and concepts form not because of individual decision, but out of a blind and shapeless hunger for new meaning, the Diggers not only gave themselves a name and a collective identity; they constructed for themselves a personified Digger; they 'created' a kind of animate Digger-doll, someone who could stand as believable evidence that all their suffering might possibly have had some sense to it. Sir John Monash, their commander in Europe hadn't suited this purpose; they were proud that (if only by 1918)

Australians were at last allowed to have their own commander, rather than a British general, and they respected what they believed to be his efficiency, and his concern for their lives and comfort, contrasting this with what trench wisdom spoke of as the murderous blunders of British staff officers in 1916 and 1917; but Monash was no 'Digger'. He was a civil engineer who knew how to conceal the madness of decision behind a style of lucid and rational calculation; as soon as the soldiers were demobilised he accepted the patriotic task of turning Victorian brown coal into Victorian electricity, so that Victoria would no longer suffer the shame of relying for coal on New South Wales, and he presided over all the bold errors of that extravagant venture with the coolness and deceit of one who could look as if he knew what he was doing equally well in peace or war.

The Diggers could also have looked among the famous VC heroes, but the most effective thematic use for them was that they should come down in the world, thus dramatising that sense of betrayal (of which the prime image was the legless, beribboned hero selling bootlaces in the street) that was one of the post-war moods of the Diggers, as it was of ex-servicemen in all the countries that had fought the war. The person the Diggers chose to turn into a representation of themselves, giving meaning to their suffering, was W. M. Hughes. And they named him after themselves. They called him 'the little Digger'.

On the night after the Peace Treaty was signed at Versailles there was a grand ball at the Majestic Hotel in Paris where Hughes had been staying; in the small hours he crossed the Channel and when he arrived at Victoria Station some waiting Diggers mobbed him—he was nursing Helen, now in her fourth year—hoisted him shoulder high, put a slouch hat on his head and carried father and baby down Victoria Street to the Anzac Buffet where a swarm of Diggers were celebrating. When Garran, his solicitor-general, restored Hughes to his wife and Helen to her nurse, eighteen cheering Diggers clung to the car as it drove off, weighted down mudguards scraping the tyres, and went to his house in Hampstead for cups of tea and glasses of beer. Two months later, back home, Hughes was once again cheered at all the train stops from Perth to Melbourne, above all by the soldiers acclaiming their 'little Digger' as they carried him on their shoulders. After that soldiers gave him a conqueror's triumph at every city and town he visited.

For the rest of his life his person was to have the ability to recapture, for those who had suffered through the war and the peace, the buoyant memories of a brief time of victory and pride. When any occasion demanded, he could be 'the little Digger' putting on his slouch hat, and when he did this, men would join together and cheer. When he died in 1952, he was to provide Australia's most famous funeral. There were daily bulletins...he was in a coma...he had rallied...he had taken a little fruit and steamed fish...he had called for the newspapers to read about his illness...he was making steady progress...he had spent a short time on the verandah in the sun...he had died peacefully, after midnight, in his sleep. The funeral of 'this: greatest of Australians', with the flag-draped coffin on the gun carriage, the three-kilometre procession of mourners, the 450,000 spectators, was a conqueror's last triumph.

***

Hughes had been the soldiers' greatest barracker: they felt he was on their side. When the war was over he was their equivalent of a Winged Victory. He had earned their tribute in that, in London, in 1918, instead of limelighting himself in British domestic politics as he had done in 1916, he limited himself to Australian affairs; to the soldiers he presented himself as the little man who was battling for *them*. Like an experienced trades union secretary, he fought for better conditions for his men: he got them the right to two months' leave in Australia—the first 6,000 went home in September—and the right to a full month's rest after a major action; he also gained the right to have the High Command consult him before the Australians were again used in a major offensive. And like an experienced trades union secretary, he made sure the men realised what he was doing for them. As a politician who knew how to nurse a constituency, he moved around the Australian troops and the word spread that Billy Hughes cared. He organised seven press parties from London to visit the troops and the blasted villages and cratered fields, the tree splinters and thistles, where they had won their fame, and, old street corner spruiker that he was, wherever there were Australian soldiers, he made a speech. And, acting like a government minister who can seem to be getting things moving, when the war was over he appeared to be using his position in London to hasten sending the troops home—to an Australia he had made more important.

Just as the soldiers, by their conduct in battle, were seen as creating a nation, Hughes, for the twelve months from June 1918 to June 1919, put on a one-man show (in the spirit of 'Australia Will Be There') demonstrating that Australia had taken its place among the nations. At first he made much of his membership of the Imperial War Cabinet, then, with fury, he raised the pitch, denouncing lack of consultation over peace terms and demanding a right for Australia to be at the peace conference. In Paris, putting on small, but much anecdotalised shows, and by playing the press, he fought among the great powers for what he saw as Australia's true interests. When everything was over, and he made his speech in parliament explaining what all the slaughter and destruction had been for, he said in effect that the valour of the Australian soldiers in France and Palestine had meant that he could take a seat at the peace conference, thus confirming Australian nationhood and preserving Australia's interest.

It was not only what he had achieved (or seemed to have achieved) that turned W. M. Hughes into the Little Digger. It was the way he went about it. His style symbolised the right values. To the Diggers he was full of spunk and able to stand up to authority; they liked his bounce and self-assertiveness, and the crude and sardonic anecdotes about his effrontery. The legends of his early days in Australia became a part of this saga. Billy Hughes was a cheeky little bugger, a real battler. Some of the very characteristics that made him so distrusted or even hated amongst the powerful or the polite were those that turned him into a folk hero for the soldiers. His own government opposed the idea of Australia having separate representation at the peace conference; many Nationalists were appalled at what seemed his disloyal attacks on the allies; Latham, Cook's adviser in Paris, loathed Hughes's assertiveness and several years later was to attempt his political assassination. But this image of the indomitable little man battling away in the Old World against its mighty powers added to the image of a national hero who personified victory, and a folk hero personifying the suppressed fantasies of the people. After his death, there was an honouring not only of the nation, but of the folk; some of the old Diggers wore their medals and their sprigs of rosemary—a few even put on their slouch hats—when they shuffled past the body as it lay in state, or saluted it as it passed by on the gun carriage. And the reporters were able to get some of them to say that they were saying goodbye to an old cobber.

Like Anzac Day itself, the Little Digger represented both authority and rebellion. Or to put it another way, he represented a taming of rebellion: although rebellion was accepted as part of the national myth, it was only in play. In September 1918, seven Australian battalions in France had mutinied against a British direction that they be broken up, to strengthen other battalions: in protest the men sent their officers away and for several days *ran themselves,* without officers, and they asked to go into action as self-controlled units. A fortnight later army diplomacy prevailed and when they were safely in rest areas, the battalions were talked into disbanding. This remarkable example of initiative and independence was not extolled from pulpit and dais on Anzac Day, but its memory was in the hearts of some of the Diggers and it was in such memories that some could give private meaning to the ceremonies, and to their image of Hughes.

They were misled. Hughes was not a rebel against authority; he was an indomitable gatecrasher of authority, wanting more of it himself. ('Only one man can govern a country, or at the best, two or three.') Even less, was he either a practitioner or an ideologue of mateship. He was an egoist so self-centred that when faced with situations that might seem to require co-operation he was often rendered impotent. He was usually incapable of either loyal co-operation with a leader or co-operation between equals; when he became prime minister he showed himself so disastrously incapable of ensuring co-operation with others that Australia was in tumult for most of that relatively brief part of his wartime prime ministership he spent in Australia; Australia had its rest periods when Hughes was out of the country. His political style was auto-erotic: to excite himself to the point of performing some action, he usually had to do it all himself. His characteristic method, the *coup,* was the way he kept things in his own hands. Because he was able to form co-operative relationships with almost no one, wherever possible—and often where almost everyone else would have found it impossible—he acted out dramas in public; he could avoid the embarrassments of dealing with individuals by addressing the people collectively as an anonymous mass, and thereby, incidentally, transferring some of his own turbulence onto the country as a whole.

However, the Diggers needed someone who personified cheekiness and comradeship, and they found him in Hughes—partly because his impotence at comradeship had given him such a turbulent and unpredictable style that it could seem that of a rebel; partly because, as someone who avoided the embarrassments of the personal by dealing with people in the mass, Hughes had maintained some of the external manners of comradeship and could project an aura of informality—even if much of this existed only in the beholders' eyes. (He didn't use the word 'brother' as obsessively as the legends suggested; he found the word 'Billy' an assault on his dignity; and much of his apparent informality may have come from sarcasm and general rudeness rather than from a view of all humans as equals.) But there was also in him something not found in the more politely self-righteous—a sense of compassion for human frailty, that came from a kind of sardonic desperation. He expected so little of the world that he could readily forgive others their sinning, except those who sinned against him. He wanted to be a statesman. He did not want to be a prig.

Hughes was not the only politician whose private reality did not match the views the public had of him. There is always a difference between a politician's secret and official faces; the public language of politics is necessarily cast into concepts more idealistic and more rational than the rivalries, the muddles, the mysteries, the illusory rituals, the boredoms and the continued unexpected interruptions of political life. Politicians who, behind the scenes, use exactly the same language they use in public are seen by their fellow politicians either as mad, or as inscrutable rogues. What was remarkable about Hughes was that what was seen as his public face became, along with the rituals and rhetoric, the badges and monuments and secret signs, part of a new national legend which purported to explain and justify Australia.

This happens to some politicians, but not to many. One of the looked-for functions of politicians is representing principles of good and evil for the rest of us, but legendary proportions are likely only in legendary times. In such periods those previously seen as crackpots can become heroes; Churchill, for example, by the 1930s was regarded by many as an eccentric has-been. But when times are cracked, the crackpot can become king. Even somewhat shadowy people, perhaps as uncertain of themselves as of life in general, can be turned, by our desires at a time of crisis, into national figures. John Curtin, unconfident and fretful if also shrewd, sensitive and humanitarian, is enlarged in our memory, if by now perhaps mistily and distantly, as a remarkable Australian, yet his main offering was that, unlike the imperial Menzies who knew only the language of empire, he could speak the language of national patriotism, if very modestly and cautiously. Unlike Hughes, who was, however, the greater 'national figure', Curtin could speak the language of unity and nurse the labour movement, and he was able to keep his tantrums as a private matter, whereas Hughes turned his tantrums into a patriotic necessity.

The Great War and its peace-making were a time for legends, and the Diggers needing a folk hero created out of Hughes something better than Hughes himself knew. The irony is not that the private reality of Hughes the politician was different from the public legend of Hughes the statesman—what else would one expect?—but that although Hughes by 1918 and 1919 was acting like one intending to be transformed into a national hero, the particular transformation was not what he had imagined. He was turned not only into the defender of empire and the protector of a White Australia with its defence ramparts in New Guinea—which was what he had intended—he was also turned into the democratic image of the soldiers themselves, and this, in a way, differed from what he had intended. For the rest of his life he got both his reward, and his punishment. Wherever he went, he would be recognised, and by those who loved the memories of the war, he would be acclaimed, but even if in his deafness he might only see their lips moving, he would know they were not acclaiming W. M. Hughes, architect of war and peace. They were acclaiming a clown like themselves; 'Look!' they would say, 'There's Billy Hughes! Good-day, Billy! Eh, good-day, Billy!

***

His other, and contrary, role in legend—that of the Labor Party's Satan, its blackest fallen angel—is likely to outlast the legend of the nation-sustainer, imperial patriot and folk hero. There may not be many more Australians who feel the need to celebrate the downfall of the Kaiser and the Turkish Emperor and folk representations were to become ambivalent enough to include Norman Gunston and Dame Edna Everage, but the Labor Party will go on needing a collective memory of how degenerate a renegade can be. Labor people can still reassure themselves of their own virtue by laying ritual curses on the memory of Billy Hughes. Yet, even here, there are differences between Hughes and the legends about him. He was not a typical Labor renegade.

For one thing, when he left the Labor Party, the times were beyond parallel. Most of the tensions in the Australian Labor Party in 1916 came from the conflicting attitudes towards the war that affected social democratic parties in all the belligerent nations. But Australia was the only country with a social democratic party in government. That military recruitment was voluntary had been a face-saver, but with the conscription referendum the social-democratic tensions emerged more openly in Australia than in any other country at that time. Whatever Hughes's intentions in precipitating it, holding such a referendum at a period of such hysteria may be seen as a remarkable democratic achievement. Despite censorship and coercion, the referendum exposed and made 'official', popular attitudes about the war and disputes about how it should be fought, and it did this in a way that happened in no other country. How could the Labor Party not have split?

Into this climate comes Hughes, besotted with the war's excitements, elated by his lionising in Britain, and susceptible to pressures (enticements also?) in both Britain and Australia to increase Australian supplies of cannon fodder (and perhaps also wondering how to win the next election). He has not the faintest talent in acting like a conciliatory national leader; if the thought had occurred to him, it might have seemed a kind of treachery to the war. So, in this explosive atmosphere, little Hughes lights a match. That may make him a fool, or (more flatteringly) a rogue, but it doesn't make him the archetypal Labor rat. The archetypal Labor renegade is the public figure who defects from the party which has been his stepping stone to power, because he has already abandoned belief in its whole dynamic. This was true of Holman and others in the defections of 1916; it was true of the defections of 1931 when Joe Lyons left the party to become leader of the United Australia Party, which was simply the Nationalist Party repainted with some fresh lettering on the front door; and it was true of the 'grouper' departures of the mid-1950s. It was not true of W. M. Hughes.

Labor ideologues can make it seem true by painting a picture of a 'real Labor Party man' as a militant socialist, and then comparing Hughes with this ideal figure. But in fact, Hughes *was* a real Labor Party man and a militant socialist was not a typical Labor Party man. As a union official Hughes tried to keep his unions out of trouble; he trusted in arbitration and concentrated on material gains, and this is exactly what most Labor Party people want union officials to do. Both in forming his unions and in fighting their battles Hughes was a brilliant manipulator of union victories. It is true that he began to enjoy greater material comfort than did members of his unions and most of his party's branches; but so do most trades union officials and Labor MPs. It is true that he worked within the capitalist system, but so do most Labor politicians. Unlike most other Labor politicians he at least had a theory about how socialism would come, and unlike any other leader of the Labor Party he constructed in his *The Case for Labor* articles in the *Daily Telegraph* a relatively coherent system of belief for an Australian Labor Party. Hughes maintained enough of his convictions as a convinced, if moderate, State socialist to see human enlightenment mainly dependent on increased government initiatives; he believed that the task of progressive government was to work through an agreed program of setting up new government agencies and starting new government interventions. That was the ordinary Labor Party ideal. As a moderate State socialist and centralist, Hughes made more efforts for significant constitutional amendments than any other Australian. Even as a captive of the Nationalists, he manoeuvred them in 1919 into supporting a referendum for wider, if temporary, Commonwealth powers; and then, in the manner of adversary politics the Labor Party questioned the referendum—because Hughes proposed it.

Hughes had been an active Labor Party man; those who see his policies as too moderate (and it should be remembered that they included the nationalisation of monopolies, trusts and combines) should criticise not Hughes but the Labor Party. In the 'khaki election' in 1919 he was still looking for a personal victory so immense that it might have given him enough power over his own party to put up a 'middle road' plan for government initiatives; apart from the war bombast in his election speeches there were appeals to the application of intelligence to economic affairs. But the Country Party had now erupted into federal politics, confusing the issues, and that had taken from him a workable majority. His own party distrusted him and he was deprived of the Labor Party's programmatic approach; he could find nothing else that would get him going. He was a successful advocate who, as he approached the age of sixty, had lost his most familiar type of brief. Insofar as he tried to act at all, not simply filling in time telling stories about how he won the war, he would still sometimes try to act like a Labor man—he did manage to set up a government oil refinery, and had a few other minor victories—but by himself he was no longer much good at thinking of things to do: he needed other people's programs to work from, and now he was leader of a party which simply wanted to return to normal. As a creative politician, Hughes very largely ceased to exist.

His successor, S. M. Bruce, left a pen picture of how sterile Hughes's errant activity had become once meaning drained away. (Although Bruce, of course, had an interest in denigrating Hughes.) Ministers would meet in cabinet, but nothing would come out of their meetings. Hughes would arrive anything up to half an hour late and, with no agenda he would then just chat about his latest enthusiasm: the purpose of the cabinet meeting would become the task of trying to talk Hughes out of his latest mad scheme. Bruce introduced the idea of the cabinet using an agenda but Hughes would still arrive late; then he would ignore the agenda, or pick around it like a hen pecking corn, discussing merely what took his fancy. When they suggested that the most senior minister present might chair a meeting if Hughes was late, he agreed, but he soon fell into the habit of undoing whatever had been done before his arrival.

***

There was one range of action that still suited Hughes for a while, and one in which he could seem the pioneer: playing a part in the public drama of Australia having a separate voice in the councils of the nations. His dramatisation of an independent Australia at the Paris Peace Conference had been one of his greatest theatrical achievements. He sustained it in his best trades union official's style. He threw up a wide ambit of claims and talked each of them up big until just before the end, when he settled for what he could get. Sometimes, when he worked on papers prepared by Garran or Latham, he argued with a trenchant comprehensiveness, stabbing at complexity, point by point. At other times, like a clever advocate, he dramatised just one simple aspect of a case: for his assault on New Guinea he sent Garran off to find a map that had Australia in the centre of it, so that he could weave a simple story around that. On occasion he just rambled, but even when he was incoherent, he was incoherent with a loud determination. With the help of two Australian journalists, he skilfully planted stories in the London and Paris press, and in one area at issue he brought pressure on President Wilson's entourage by successfully playing on United States' newspapers as well. He could use the union leader's language of the walkout—he threatened not to sign the peace treaty if Australia failed in its claims on Nauru's phosphate—and he sparked off one of the conference's most outrageous anecdotes, the anecdote of a shocked President Wilson leaning forward at a meeting of the Council of Ten and asking, 'Mr Hughes, am I to understand that if the whole civilised world asked Australia to agree to a mandate in respect of these islands, Australia is prepared to defy the appeal to the whole civilised world?', whereupon the gnome-like Hughes, after some stage business with his hearing aid, replied 'That's about the size of it, Mr President'. The anecdote may not be true—it may even have been concocted in the Wilson camp—but it became an honoured part of the Hughes legend. When it was all over although Hughes hadn't got all he wanted and, indeed, saw part of his cause defeated he, again like a good trades union official, polished up what had been done and presented it as a famous victory.

On New Guinea and Nauru he had hoped for outright annexation—in New Guinea he got most of what he wanted, which was to keep other nations out, both in immigration and trade, but he was shocked by British greed in insisting on sharing the spoils of Nauru. As one who had accepted the leftist critique of the war as a trade war, then used the fact that the victors could gain the spoils, as he did in his Wake Up England speeches in 1916, as a strong reason for supporting the war, he felt a high principled sense of injustice that his attempt to impose larger reparations on Germany failed; he saw Australia as cheated—it had risked a lot of money on the war without getting its investment back, let alone making a profit. It was Hughes's victory, and his alone, to gain Wilson's co-operation in blocking the Japanese in attempting to include a statement of the principle of race equality in the preamble of the covenant of the League of Nations; as a true White Australian Hughes saw this as a significant victory, but with his tragic view of a world in which matters were settled by might, not right, the forming of the League of Nations itself seemed a defeat. In his 'realism' Hughes was naive enough to believe that there could be an armed alliance between Britain and the United States, perhaps with the French in it as well, and only this could guarantee a victor's peace in a victor's world.

Yet in no time at all, it was only Australia's separate participation in League of Nations meetings that was left of the mirage of Australian independence. Hughes had put on his show in Paris, and the anecdotes lasted—his wisecracks with Clemenceau, his rebukes of Wilson, his uses of deaf aid diplomacy, his quarrels with Lloyd George suggesting that at least for a short period of festival, Australia *was* seen as a nation and that Hughes had done it. Then it was all finished. At the 1921 Imperial Conference Hughes attempted a revival season, by demanding separate representation for Australia at the Washington Conference on naval strengths in the Pacific. But because the United States wouldn't agree, he lost. That was the end of the public drama of Australia's independent nationhood.

The public drama of Australia playing its rightful role in world diplomacy would not be seen again for a generation, until H. V. Evatt took it up in World War II, but in that between-wars period of RSL badges and Anzac patriotism what remained for Hughes was to be seen as the embodiment of a certain view of Australian *Realpolitik* and in the 1930s as the dictators took over more and more time on the cinema newsreels it could seem to many people a very likely one. It was founded on Hughes's vision of a world in which only brute force could settle human affairs and in which, in the last resort, disputes between nations would be decided by blood and iron.

But such a vision, as well as affronting all pacifists, could, if it mentioned specific threats, also confound many conservatives. In the 1930s, right up to the eve of the Nazi attack on Poland, most conservative political leaders, unlike Hughes, were to play down the Japanese, then the Italian, then the German aggressions. The idea of an immediate and *explicit* military threat to Australia became an active part of the conservative political repertoire only with the Cold War. In the meantime, the threat to be dramatised was *the enemy within*.

Hughes did important pioneer work in developing the theme of a bolshevism that now had the Labor Party in its grip. *The Labor Party was committed to a policy of communism. That was the beginning and end of it. It proposed to set up a replica of the Soviet government of Russia. When he had led the Labor Party it was loyal. Now it was impregnated with the foul doctrines of bolshevism. The party had been turned from the great purpose for which it was created to purposes infinitely mean, treacherous and base.* The Labor Party's bolshevism was a rhetorical device worked by Hughes to overcome the difficulty of maintaining the reality of a world of threat while practically no one in the conservative political parties had any plans for Australian defence (except in illusion, for party advantage, at election time). With it went what Hughes presented as Labor's historic defeatism: *The electors knew them to be men who when the clouds of war were darkest counselled peace by negotiation with a victorious enemy. If Labor had had its way victory would never have come to us. We would have lost everything. Our national honour would have been dragged through the mire. The White Australia Policy would have been abandoned. We would have suffered, in one blow, the destruction of everything we loved and valued. The fair name of Australia would have been a thing at which men would have spat.*

The language of national independence in strategic policy had been something Hughes had brought with him from the Labor Party; it distressed most of his new political allies and he lacked the political strength, the conceptual power and the administrative vigour to do anything about it. He fell back on the suggestion that Australia gained its independence through the strength of the empire: *the nations of the world had committed Australia to their councils on a footing of equality, but Australia was a nation only by the grace of God and the power of the British Empire. When the voice of Australia spoke as part of the British Empire with its 500 million of people, its mighty navy, its flag on every sea, its strongholds on every continent, its power and its glory shining and splendid, acknowledged by all, then she spoke in trumpet tones that were heard and heeded throughout all the earth. This Australia of ours could not stand, could not progress, could not exist, unless it was an integral part of the Empire.* Privately, after what he had seen of the British leadership, Hughes was sceptical about both British honesty and British nerve; but politicians do not normally express private doubts about beliefs that in public receive the loudest claps.

Formulas of this kind, employed by Hughes in the 1919 and 1922 elections, were to serve the conservatives for decades. The conservatives could now run down defences and be as lacking in military talents and imagination as the Labor Party, but they could distinguish themselves by pulling the stern faces of men who were *realists*. They could appear to be realists because they had 'won the war' and because they could sometimes speak the language of pessimism, but above all because it was they who asserted that not only honour but a hard-headed appreciation of brute fact meant that Australian security depended absolutely on loyalty to those who were later to become known as *great and powerful friends*.

Chapter 6

Old Billy

In November 1920, Hughes sat with knights, generals, brigadiers and a number of prominent citizens on a platform in the King's Hall in Sydney to receive a casket made of Australian blackwood. Inside was an illuminated address expressing thanks for the 'fidelity, courage and determination he had shown in the fight for human freedom and traditions of the British race'. Two brigadiers delivered eulogies and the crowd sang 'For he's a jolly good fellow'. When he spoke, Hughes rewarded them by recalling *the dark days in which the Empire had stood firm*, and, looking to the future, *the world-wide conspiracy against this Empire of ours* against which *it was no use fighting with gloves on; one must fight with bare fists*. Accompanying the blackwood casket and the illuminated address was a cheque for £25,000.

The next day he addressed a conference of the Nationalist Party. He reminded them that in his early days in Sydney he had slept in the Domain for three nights and had nothing to eat. He urged the conference to set itself against hare-brained bolsheviks and red raggers, but he also warned them that their party was rumoured to be bolstering up the capitalists: as for him, he would never seek to erect a rampart to shelter great vested interests. Already, on that day, however, there had been a question in parliament about the cheque for £25,000, asking for details of the lists of those thankful citizens who had donated the money. The donation lists were never to be revealed, although the most favoured guess is that most of the money was raised by the 'Broken Hillionaire', W. S. Robinson whom Hughes had first fought with and then befriended at the time of the breaking up of the German metal combine and who now wrote to Hughes so frankly that Hughes would burn his letters after he had read them. For the rest of his life, Hughes's enemies, including those in his own party, were to speculate as to which great vested interests had rewarded him—at a particularly convenient time, because at that stage he was nearly bankrupt. (When he died in 1952, he was worth £70,000.)

As Hughes's prime ministership continued, rumours suggested that some of those putting money into the National Party through these secret committees that financed it wanted to get rid of him. According to one rumour, the shipping interests wanted to see the Commonwealth Shipping Line established by Hughes destroyed, or at least controlled. To that purpose, they were investing in the newly-established Country Party. In other rumours, importers and those with landed interests were unhappy with tariff increases and the increasing support for manufacturing shown in Hughes's speeches. There were rumoured to have been two special meetings to express discontent with Hughes's failure to take an intelligent and sympathetic interest in the needs of businessmen; the first of these meetings was said to have resulted in the appointment as treasurer of S. M. Bruce, scion of a family of Melbourne soft goods merchants, a gentleman, smoothly born to rule. Some newspapers were becoming hostile to Hughes. Early in 1922 he toured several States to try to answer criticism within the State parties and among their backers, but by the middle of the year he was approaching one of those health breakdowns from which he never seemed far away. His own parliamentary party was again becoming cantankerous. Party meetings were as barren as cabinet meetings.

When the election came at the end of 1922 many of Hughes's enemies on his own side of the fence were publicly out to get him. The *Age* attacked *the secret little body of rich men* behind Hughes; Sir William Watt, who had held the fort for him in the sixteen months he spent in London in 1918 and 1919 but had broken with Hughes after a quarrel in 1920, attacked his *mistaken tactics and lack of judgment* and called for *an end to hectic politics and the beginning of a time of quiet, creative statesmanship;* Earle Page, the leader of the new Country Party, called for the replacement of Hughes's *thinly disguised socialism and theatrical posturing with a return to the clean government of those who believed in self reliance, individual enterprise and private initiative;* Latham, spokesman for a new party in Victoria which was intended to put everything back where it was before 1916, attacked a government that was *neither Liberal nor Socialist but was inefficient, recklessly extravagant and politically demoralising to a degree never before experienced in Australia, guilty of appalling waste of public funds, hopeless ineptitude and incompetence, grossly irregular procedures and a ruinous policy of shipbuilding and shipowning and excessive taxation with a leader who, in a wholly improper and pernicious act, had accepted a cheque of £25,000.* Neither the Country Party nor Latham's party did as well in the elections as they had expected. But the Nationalists now depended absolutely on Country Party support. Hughes was finished.

His execution took nearly eight weeks. Advised by Latham, whose loathing of Hughes went back to the Paris Peace Conference and to earlier hatreds in London, Page used the Country Party's fourteen seats in the house of representatives to enforce an absolute veto on Hughes as prime minister. Over the better part of summer the formalities were dealt with—the meetings of party managers, the firm party resolutions, the confident statements, the press headlines. Suddenly, only two days after a vote of support from his own party, and a breaking off of negotiations, Hughes gave in. Unlike Hughes, Bruce commanded bridge games by winning points with a cool brilliance and he kept a low handicap on the golf course: earlier he had committed his loyalty to Hughes; now he had won Hughes's job as prime minister.

Yet to Hughes this could seem merely one small aberration in a long game:... surely the new Bruce-Page government could not last... they were mere amateurs... only two of them had been in government before... they would stumble into some quick disaster... then W. M. Hughes would return to his rightful place at the table... Meanwhile he could spend more time with Helen, now aged seven.

Hughes was sixty. Nearly twenty-nine years of parliamentary life lay behind him, yet slightly more than half of his parliamentary life still lay ahead. He would not become prime minister again, but he would run it close, and he would help destroy two other prime ministers. He would be the little Digger, a revered living legend, the mascot of a generation of veterans. He would also be one of the closest and keenest of party infighters, a man who believed that only he should be prime minister.

He would go on being a statesman of the mouth, an orator, to whom speeches were reality. The preparation of one of his big speeches would still be a new creation of the world, but carried out much less calmly than God's creation. His staff would draft and redraft, sometimes for a month or more. He would tear up the drafts, throw the pieces on the floor, demand that they be put together again; he would never say what he wanted, merely reject everything that was offered; in the last moments of hysteria before a speech was made he might still be altering drafts, perhaps restoring some of his most trusted clichés. When it was over, for a day or so, he might be cheerful and calm, although not likely to give any thanks to those who had helped bring his relief.

He would again enjoy office—any office... minister for health, minister for repatriation, vice-president of the executive council, minister for external affairs, attorney general, minister for industry, minister for the navy...he would be all of these, some of them several times over, absorbing himself in each of them, devoting himself to it, and trying to bring something to it by his own method of obsessive rage. His quarrels with his staff would finally become a national legend, but some of his staff respected him. They knew that he could speak softly and politely for at least part of the day. They could recognise that he knew a lot, perhaps even that part of his restlessness came from seeking novelty and vision, but not usually finding it; that this cursing could be a way of working up to the right phrase and his anger could be used positively, not only as a drive to action, but as a tragic means of securing detachment and contemplating folly; and that in his sardonic world, although he was unable to express thanks, he was remarkably able to forgive human failings—but not when they were a cause of frustration to him. At the age of ninety he would approach death still fretful that he had not again been made attorney-general.

At the beginning of 1923, after his sacking, he began planning his comeback, by returning to one of the places where he had started—writing articles for the *Daily Telegraph*. But they did not attract the attention gained, a generation before, by *The Case for Labor*. There was no sudden wave of enthusiasm for W. M. Hughes... He went on a lecture tour in the United States...He bought a bungalow at Lindfield, near his new constituency of North Sydney, Bendigo having become too hard to hold...He took up golf, which he played as a great adventure, enlivened by chances for cheating and pocketing other people's golf balls...He lived among some of Australia's richest and most polite people, but he didn't make friends of any of them, preferring to play golf or billiards with the tough and self-made.

He had to wait for six-and-a-half years before he could destroy Bruce and in this time, in one of the ironies of politics, Bruce was able to bring in more measures of government enterprise than Hughes achieved after the Great War, although it was Hughes who had been distrusted for his 'socialism'. Bruce was given to intelligent visions of rational behaviour, with the central government providing a carefully planned superstructure for private economic development. One of his favourite political forms was the commission of inquiry: some of the practical results of his plans were so ludicrous that if his had been a Labor government they would have been unmasked as socialist extravagance, but Bruce, when one plan failed, would calmly set up another commission. Yet along with his ability to preside over fiasco with great reasonableness and, on other occasions, to preside modestly over an intelligent success, there was also an urge to violence that found expression in 'law and order' campaigns.

He won a law-and-order election against the bolshevik menace in 1925. The campaign was a masterpiece in techniques useful in gaining both votes and financial support; but he then made the error of taking his own campaign too seriously. It could be politically worthwhile to use strong language against the union movement; it could be dangerous to put the language into effect. Bruce's obsession with the unions undid him, and Hughes, who for six years had presumably thought of little else, was now able to gain his revenge.

Bruce came out of the 1928 election with a small coalition majority that began to break up not long after he had assembled it. Early in 1929 he feared that Hughes might bring him down with a stop-gap government over the issue of his selling the Commonwealth Shipping Line Hughes had set up. But Hughes had cast himself as defender of another form of righteousness: he would champion the arbitration system and the trades union movement against the 'industrial civil war' that, he said, Bruce was now creating in Australia, with his proposal that the national government vacate arbitration, leaving it to the States.

Hughes put himself forward as a man of principle *who did not believe there was one law for labour and a different law for capital or that penalties and punishments alone would bring industrial peace*: he pictured Bruce as a man who was not prepared to enforce the law impartially and as a trouble-making destroyer of the people's institutions. It was such a successful reprise of the performance of Will Hughes, Labor stalwart, that even Frank Anstey, a Labor MP who had specialised in attacking Hughes's renegadism, now praised him: *Hughes had developed in hunger and poverty and misery; poor workmen had lifted him up on their bucklers to the most honoured position in the country and in the arbitration laws there was evidence of his driving force, some of his blood, his brain, his talents. Now in spite of his present associations, he could not forget the things of his early manhood.*

It was the greatest act of destruction in national politics performed by just one man. Clothing himself in a form of righteousness summoned from his past, Hughes became principal figure in a long parliamentary drama that, member by member, shook away the government's majority. Most of this was not connected with the direct occasion for Bruce's downfall. The greatest preliminary act of parliamentary theatre was a week long no-confidence debate on the dropping of a prosecution against John Brown, the Newcastle coal baron, in which the government were made to look ruthless apologists for vested interests, and Hughes finally got the numbers by getting a movie distributor to telephone an MP lobbyist for the movie industry and ask him to vote against Bruce on arbitration because it was the only way to defeat Bruce's proposal for a cinema tax. The small commando group of rebels Hughes had assembled would strike at Bruce for a number of different reasons; but Hughes knew he could give it all a common meaning.

When the Nationalist Party expelled him, the time had come. He made his successful strike on 10 September 1929. At 3.55 p.m. he moved that Bruce's proposal be shelved until it was put to a referendum or an election. Five hours later Hughes had won... and was celebrating his victory with one of his rare cigarettes, and a cup of tea; in his pocket was a list of the ministry he would form, with Labor support, when the governor-general sent for him.

No governor-general would ever again send for Hughes but in the election that followed this havoc he had a sweet revenge: the Nationalists who had expelled him won only fourteen seats, only four more than the Country Party. Bruce himself was defeated but, running as an Independent Nationalist (in a £10,000 campaign financed by businessmen sympathisers), Hughes kept North Sydney on first preferences. For a week or two he waited for a call from the Labor Party, to rejoin it...

Now there were other excitements. Wall Street crashed a week after the Labor Party took office and as the whole capitalist world was falling into the misery and disasters of the depression, Hughes, whose early parliamentary speeches in 1894 drew much of their emotion from the image of the soup kitchen and the starving worker, returned to some of the 1890s street corner rhetoric of hard times—larded with more modern notions of economic policy worked out by Theodore, the Labor treasurer, with whom he had a private friendship and occasional confidential dealings. With an old Labor man's instinct, he blamed the banks. When the Bank of England, at the invitation of the Labor government, sent out Sir Otto Niemeyer to investigate the affairs of Australians and tell them what to do, Hughes joined in the radical attack on such an abject act by publishing a threepenny pamphlet exposing *the powerful influences that were at work, skilfully moulding the minds of the people. Sir Otto represented not the people of England, but great financial interests who wanted us to scrap our policy of building up Australian industries and to confine ourselves to producing raw materials for Britain. And in order to do this—which he told us was the only means of our economic salvation—we must reduce our standard of living. The causes of unemployment were deep-rooted in the system under which we lived; the welfare and progress of Australia depended upon the maintenance of a policy of encouragement of Australian industry. Low wages did not mean cheap production; what Australia wanted was not reduced wages but cheaper money, an improved and rationalised system of credit.*

At a time when the political right had fragmented into many parties, some secret, conspiratorial and quasi-military, Hughes now aged sixty-eight, in October 1930, confidently began to form a new party—the Australian Party: it would be a national organisation, 'democratic and progressive', with Hughes as president. It was launched in Chatswood Town Hall, and the next year it ran to a convention, a constitution and a policy; but money was hard to find; there were quarrels about expenses; alarmed by Hughes's radical attacks on Niemeyer, the newspapers gave the new party a bad run; Hughes was secretive about what the policy was supposed to mean and offended supporters by his autocracy, his sarcasm and his outbursts of radicalism; when the party did badly in a New South Wales state election Hughes retreated from it into the comforts of influenza. It was another new organisation, the All For Australia League, that won the premier place when its leader became Joe Lyons, who had just defected from the Labor government. A new renegade served the purposes of the conservatives more adequately than did an old one. Lyons was more comforting than Hughes with his talk about deep-rooted causes and powerful interests; Lyons offered not bold new ways but the reassurance of one who could seem as ordinary as the voters themselves. When the Nationalist Party mated with the All For Australia League, producing the United Australia Party (UAP) (with the same independent committee of business men secretly financing it as had financed the National Party), Hughes abandoned his own party, joined the UAP, and went off with his wife and Helen, now sixteen, for a long holiday in Europe and Britain.

Helen had just a touch of Hughes's high cheekbones, and a large share of his wilfulness although it was deployed with charm. She loved Hughes, and he both loved her and enjoyed the praise she brought him. As they travelled around Europe there were intimations of that other life, of a family life in retirement, but after he came back, in 1933, he had a last fling at again making himself the centre of something: he launched a Defence of Australia League in the Sydney Town Hall, but it came to nothing; so he wrote to Keith Murdoch that he would again like to be a cabinet minister. In 1934, at the age of seventy-two he became minister for health, minister for repatriation and vice-president of the executive council.

A year later he was put out of office when a book he had written, *Australia and the War Today*, clashed with the politics of the government. In this book he had again stated his tragic view of the world: *Life was a fight for survival; all government rested on force and progress itself was bought with blood. Disputes between nations were as inevitable as disputes between individuals in society and the maintenance of peace, order and the rule of law in society was absolutely dependent on force.* As in 1916 he was able to use the left-wing cry that *the cause of war is the struggle for markets* as a reason to support war, not to oppose it; in the conflict between nations Australia must defend its interests. And when the Japanese advanced into China, the Italians assaulted Abyssinia, the Germans re-armed and the League of Nations collapsed, he saw that *the world was an armed camp. We found ourselves unarmed and almost defenceless, confronting a world resounding with preparations for war. We had no fleet capable of offering an enemy serious resistance; no air force strong enough to defend us from aerial or naval attack; no land force that could protect us from invasion.*

As a prophet of the disasters that would come from European fascism and Japanese militarism, he was playing a part that few public persons were ready to play in the mid-1930s, although the dark omens were all around: It was a moment in which his whole view of the brutality of power aptly gave him a vision that others lacked; the world fitted his tragic view. But his warnings came to nothing. His vision was shared, for a period, by the communists and their sympathisers, and by some of the radicals and liberals, but he could not speak to them. It was a vision shunned by the Labor Party, where the pacifist left saw attacks on fascism as dangerous war-mongering and the Catholic right saw fascism as a check to communism, and both sides saw foreign policy as so likely to divide the party that, in the interests of party unity, it was better not to have a foreign policy. Perhaps Hughes's vision was shared by a majority of the Australian people—certainly, his words struck home amongst those Returned Men who shared his tragic view, and who were stoically bringing up their sons to fight in 'the next war'—but he was old, and, both organisationally and conceptually, he lacked the talent to pull things together in some new way. By the very harshness of its expression, his 'realism' could most offend those who might have accepted it. He could not learn to speak of hard matters softly.

The next year he was once again back in office, still itching to speak more bluntly than the rest of the government about German, Italian and Japanese military ambitions but, as a member of a government, he was choked by his own cravings for office.

His way out was to speak of national threat in terms of population policy: wanting to *write a warning in fetters of fire on the walls of the heavens* he proclaimed, wherever he could, the slogan POPULATE OR PERISH. By this means, he could be an 'alarmist', frantically sounding the tocsin against coming perils then, returning to the gentle role of cabinet minister, he could go downstairs and initial some more papers. Even as minister for health he managed to put national peril on to the health agenda: warning of falling birthrates, he launched a campaign to praise the maternal virtues. He threw himself into it with such excess that colleagues laughed at him as 'the minister for motherhood', a phrase that gave even greater poignancy to the death of Helen, whom he loved more than anything in the world: in 1937 she died in London, aged twenty-one, after an abortion.

In the same year he became minister for external affairs.

His first public duty was to read out a speech supporting those policies of diplomatic appeasement about which, in private, he could be so sarcastic. For most of the time he 'behaved himself' which meant, in particular, not provoking the German consul-general, whose complaints were taken so gravely by the government that on one occasion they temporarily shut down a Sydney radio station that had criticised the Nazis. But Hughes could feel war in the air. He lived with this excitement in a state of permanent potential conflict with colleagues who still felt that somehow 'the next war' would not come. A member of his staff recalls how Hughes was interviewed by local reporters in the lounge of a country hotel after Lyons had sent telegrams ordering his ministers to say nothing about foreign affairs: when the reporters asked Hughes what he thought of Hitler he said, 'I'm only minister for external affairs—I'm not allowed to say anything—so therefore I cannot comment. I will, of course, say that if you paved the way from here to Broken Hill with bibles, and if that man Hitler swore on oath on every one of them, I wouldn't believe a goddam bloody word he said'. Off goes Hughes. His staff spends the evening keeping this out of the newspapers.

In his writings he spoke of the interests of Australia: *When all the world was armed, Australia dared not go unarmed. We sought to molest none; to injure none; we desired only to be allowed to develop our heritage in peace. But unless we were to stand like sheep before the butcher we must, without delay, create such defence forces as would make an attack upon Australia a venture so hazardous that none would attempt it.* But, in the style of a politician, he also thought of his own interests: in Hughes's troubled vision of the future he saw himself in the middle of these coming troubles. In the silence he was keeping, he could think of a time when he would again be prime minister. He was likely to boast in private that *he had controlled armies, and broken generals. He had been part of the history of the country for fifty years; he had seen men come and go; and he liked to think that when he went it would be in an aura of greatness.* After an argument with a member of his staff about newspapers—all of which, apart from the London *Times* he saw as despicable—he recalled his old power: 'You know, there was a time when the constitution of this country was in my fountain pen'. Then, looking into the war clouds ahead: 'By God, that time is coming again, and I'll blast you and your bloody newspapers off the face of the earth'. When he was given the task of running a recruiting campaign for the volunteer reserve, it could really seem as if the old times would return: Hughes moved across the country quarrelling with his staff, making speeches to big crowds: the number of volunteers doubled; the newspapers were filling with W. M. Hughes's speeches and Billy Hughes's photographs.

At the age of seventy-six, Hughes's time almost did come again. Lyons unexpectedly died in April 1939—during a period when the political world was waiting for the next moves in R. G. Menzies's attempts to seize from him the job of prime minister—and Earle Page, destroyer of Hughes in 1923, again set about snatching the prime ministership from a man he did not like. This time it was Menzies.

Journalists would sometimes use the word 'proconsul' to describe the position of Australian high commissioner in London. All the high commissioners had been prime ministers, and it was a position that could seem the only honourable retirement. It was now held by Bruce, and Page tried to tempt him back to govern Australia. But 'proconsul' was the wrong word: London was the imperial city and Australia merely a province; Bruce declined the offer of banishment. Page's plan was a private one, unknown to most of the party. What was known as soon as the lobbying began at Joe Lyons's funeral was that Billy Hughes was again ready to be prime minister.

The lobbying for Hughes was begun by a young Sydney MP, Bill McCall, who, earlier, had worked for Hughes in his constituency, and whose son had Hughes as godfather. McCall and others worked cleverly for Hughes. In a landscape darkened by the clouds of a coming war the times had gone backwards and an old has-been could again seem the man of the hour; Hughes had the extra advantage that he was not R. G. Menzies. Menzies beat him with a majority of only four. If three MPs had changed their minds, at seventy-six W. M. Hughes would again have been prime minister of Australia.

The wounds of that contest didn't heal. In the twenty-nine months of Menzies's prime ministership, most of them months of war, and all of them months of envy, hatred and distrust within the government party and among its main backers, Hughes sat behind desks in capital cities and again acted as attorney-general (also for a while, as minister for industry and then minister for the navy). He was number two in the party and, for the period the Country Party kept up a boycott of Menzies, number two in the government. He was approaching eighty, but he still persisted—barely sleeping, barely eating—relaxing by cheating at golf, or billiards or Chinese chequers, or by driving eccentrically, or by keeping others busy, or simply by talking. He summoned the old rhetoric: *Australia was a great and rich prize at a time when the empire was in deadly peril; the day was dark, the way was long; upon the issue of this titanic struggle hung the destiny of the world.* He still spoke of the *communist menace in this great and fateful hour,* and as attorney-general set up an anticommunist front organisation (its main function was to publicize Hughes's speeches) and handled a secret fund to sponsor anti-communist activities in the unions but as soon as Hitler invaded the Soviet Union he found a justifying rhetoric for that, too: *Russia stood side by side with us fighting the enemy who had vowed the destruction of democracy,* and in one of his many returns to the little man taking on the privileged, he sneered at how *only a numerically small section, mainly composed of the very nicest people, were those who viewed the pact between Britain and Russia with distrust.* He maintained public loyalty to Menzies, but it was Hughes the little magsman who, in his gossiping, provided some of the most repeated phrases of denigration: *Menzies was long on words, but short on action... Menzies could not lead and would not follow... Menzies couldn't lead a flock of homing pigeons.*

Menzies's basic inability to look like a war-time prime minister became a scandal. A country storekeeper's son who had worked his way up in the world, he found it hard to speak a language of common patriotism in which war and death could be praised to his fellow Australians. Menzies saw honour in maintaining a lordly air of dilatoriness (that sometimes concealed a real dilatoriness, but not always), the ability to look busy, so important to Hughes, seemed demeaning to Menzies. Unable to cast the image of a diligent patriot who cared deeply about the war, Menzies almost lost the 1940 election (only the voting system saved him), and with this he lost a political leader's greatest weapon against his rivals—the belief in him as a vote winner. The whole structure of support that usually sustains a conservative party in Australian national politics was now slipping and splintering. Newspapers attacked Menzies. Business firms lobbied against him. Money from conservative backers went into the Labor Party. There were criticism and gossip in the gentlemen's clubs.

Within the parliamentary party, Bill McCall brought the party to the point where a majority was ready to push Menzies over the cliff; when, at the very last moment, unexpectedly, Menzies still tried to cling on, it was McCall who stamped on his fingers. In order to choose a new leader for the UAP, McCall became busy again, but this time there was a more general move to make Hughes leader, although for Hughes it was not a happy move: putting him in was seen by some of those who voted for him as merely a safe, stopgap arrangement. He would not be prime minister; the leadership of the government itself had passed to the Country Party leader, Artie Fadden (if only for forty days, after which support for the government collapsed and Labor took over). When better times again came to the party, they could put in someone else.

As a prize, leadership of the UAP was dead fruit, but Hughes carried it with enough conviction to provoke what he presented as the Menzies-led 'reactionary clique', who attacked the centralism which led him to urge a referendum to abolish State parliaments. In one of the many ironies of his life, Hughes then supported the moderation, patience and compromise with which John Curtin successfully extended conscription; Hughes was then attacked by the Menzies group, who preferred in a Labor government the careless boldness by which Hughes, in 1916, had failed to gain conscription, had troubled the mirages of national unity, but had broken the Labor Party. The Menzies group tried to censure Hughes for his support for Curtin; they lost by fifteen to twenty-four and they formed within the party, a self-styled 'National Service Group'. Hughes had a few more thunderbolts to throw. He attacked Menzies as *the great self seeker, the man behind the scenes in every intrigue, the great destroyer of unity* and fought the 1943 election as leader of the UAP, (although Fadden, as leader of the opposition, led the campaign and some of the conservatives still saw Menzies as leader).

Hughes had announced that he would retire from the leadership after the election. The party put Menzies back in, and appointed Hughes as deputy to *the great destroyer of unity*. Soon after, Hughes put up his last revolt. When the UAP decided to withdraw its representatives from the bi-partisan Advisory War Council, the Labor government so praised the contribution Hughes had made to this body that he withdrew his resignation, defied his party, and returned to the council. At the age of eighty-two he was again expelled from a political party.

In 1945, after the UAP had formed the Liberal Party they asked him to return. It was the sixth time he had joined a political party (two were parties he had himself formed). He was old, lonely, his back stooped, the strength gone from his voice, his concentration faltering; often now he was quiet, a little bag of bones done up in gent's natty suiting who had nothing much to say; but even if by now he had decided he might never again be prime minister—but how can one be certain?—he was still hoping for one more spell in office as attorney-general. He made speeches less often, but he still built much of his life around speech-making. He still enjoyed his ritual public appearances; for the newspapers he was still good for a Billy Hughes story. But Menzies would never trust him again, and to most of the younger people in the party he was now an improbable, if likeable, leftover from the past, an amusing mascot perhaps, but hardly an elder statesman.

Australia abounded in people who told Billy Hughes stories and gave Billy Hughes imitations at parties, but now that Hughes was stripped of all power, habits that were once excused by his genius were now seen by a younger generation as, at the best, entertaining, and, at the worst, absurd. He was reduced to something less than human size—a funny old man. To some he was a dotty old chap who had fired more than a hundred secretaries (HUGHES: *Who are you, young man?* YOUNG MAN: *I'm your new secretary, Mr Hughes.* HUGHES: You *mean you* WERE *my new secretary!*)... According to the stories, his thin little body was kept working by his masseur, who rubbed whisky into it...He was Australia's most photographed homecraftsman, posing in front of woodwork and copperware, all his own work...He ate like a bird and would even complain that the soup was tough... He was a mean old tightwad who squabbled over the household bills, alternatively he was a most generous old gentleman, and extraordinarily fond of children ... He quarrelled compulsively and incessantly with his wife *(Hey Mary, where's that bloody thing? Mary! Ah, where's that goddam woman?)* and when visiting, he warned people against her kleptomania... Above all, like one who can make himself invisible, he was a magician who, as master of his own hearing, was able to create the world or kill it, according to how he turned the knob on his little black hearing box.

He sat in parliament to the end of his life, and continued to be a meticulous parliamentarian. Driving up to

Canberra, and driving back. Taking his place in the house of representatives. Reading the notice papers. Eating with his wife and his secretary at his regular table in the Hotel Canberra. A courteous host, aware that when people met him they were meeting a great man, he would serve them famous anecdotes along with the scones and tea. Sometimes he would sit in parliament, an old man with his deaf aid turned off, looking straight ahead, busy thinking. He was initiating moves to have himself given the Order of Merit.

In 1949, at the age of eighty-seven, three years before his death his party had made him face a pre-selection. It was the first time he had been up before a party branch in this way since the pre-selection ballot in 1894, when he had stood outside a hall on the waterfront, waiting to see if they would choose him as a candidate for parliament. ('You've been selected. Run for your life!') It had been a favourite anecdote, one he told other prime ministers. Now here he was again, in the party rooms, waiting to make a short speech in front of a committee, most of whom had not been born when he first ran for parliament. He was in good form. He stood outside with the other candidates, as joking and sprightly as if it were fifty-five years before and he was starting all over again...

Acknowledgements

◆ The official biography of Hughes, by L. F. Fitzhardinge, is in two parts: Vol. I, *The Fiery Particle* (1862-1914) has been reissued by Angus & Robertson in paperback; Vol. 2, *The Little Digger* (Angus & Robertson) was published in 1978. In *Billy Hughes in Paris: The Birth of Australian Diplomacy* (Nelson, 1978), W.J. Hudson has written an account, both brief and excellent, of Hughes at the Paris Peace Conference. W. Farmer Whyte, *William Morris Hughes: his Life and Times* (1957) is rambling and unreliable. F. C. Browne, *They Called Him Billy* (1945) is little more than a collection of unassessed Hughes anecdotes.

The main books written by Hughes himself are *The Case for Labor* (1910, reprinted 1970), a selection of his labour movement rhetoric, *The Day—and After* (1916), a selection of his imperial rhetoric, *The Splendid Adventure* (1929) and *Australia and the War Today* (1935). His two collections of anecdotes about himself are *Crusts and Crusades* (1947) and *Policies and Potentates* (1950). The two books glamorising him after his 1916 speeches in Britain are D. Sladen, *From Boundary Rider to Prime Minister* (1916) and S. W. Sprigg, *W. M. Hughes, The Strong Man of Australia* (1916).

In looking for leads about the beginnings of the Labor Party in Sydney I found Patrick Ford, *Cardinal Moran and the A.L.P.* (1966) particularly useful. Also useful were D.J. Murphy (ed), *Labor in Politics: the state labor parties in Australia, 1880-1920* (1975), P. Loveday, A. W. Martin &

R. S. Parker (eds), *The Emergence of the Australian Party System* (1977) and Bede Nairn, *Civilising Capitalism (1973)*. For the labour movement in the first two decades of the twentieth century, Ian Turner, *Industrial Labour and Politics: the Dynamics of the Labour Movement in Eastern Australia, 1900-1921* (1965).

Of biographies and memoirs, I consulted G. F. Pearce, *Carpenter to Cabinet: Thirty Seven Years of Parliament* (1951), H.V. Evatt, *Australian Labour Leader: the Story of W. A. Holman and the Labour Movement* (1942, republished as a paperback, 1978), Peter Heydon, *Quiet Decision: a Study of George Foster Pearce* (1965), Cecil Edwards, *Bruce of Melbourne* (1965), R. R. Garran, *Prosper the Commonwealth* (1958), J. A. La Nauze, *Alfred Deakin* (1965, republished as a paperback, 1978). J. Thompson, *On Lips of Living Man* (1962) was particularly useful.

On the Great War, I found some new ideas in Marc Ferro, *The Great War, 1914-1918* (trans. by Nicole Stone, 1973). For the Australian story I used various volumes of C. E. W. Bean's *Official History of Australia in the War of 1914-18*, with a touch of his *Anzac to Amiens* (1946) and some reference to Bill Gammage, *The Broken Years* (1975). On the home front: Ernest Scott, *Australia During the War* (1938), vol xi of the *Official History*, L. C. Jauncey, *The Story of Conscription in Australia* (1935, republished in 1968 with a foreword by P. O'Farrell) and Ian Turner, *Sydney's Burning* (1967).

Of journal articles those that I found particularly useful were Murray Perks, 'Labor and the Governor-General's Recruiting Conference', *Labour History* (No 34, May 1978), Stephen Murray-Smith, 'On the Conscription Trail: The Second Referendum seen from beside W. M. Hughes', *Labour History* (No 33, November 1977) and Michael McKernan, 'Catholics, conscription and Archbishop Mannix', *Historical Studies* (No 68, April 1977).

Other journal articles consulted included D. W. Rawson, 'Labour, Socialism and the Working Class', *Australian*

Journal of Philosophy and History (Vol 7, No 1, 1961), P.J. O'Farrell, 'The Australian Socialist League and the Labor Movement, 1887-1891', *Historical Studies* (No 30, 1958), L. G. Churchward, 'The American Influence on the Australian Labor Movement', *Historical Studies* (No 19, 1952), F. Picard, 'Henry George and the Labor Split of 1891', *Historical Studies* (No 21, 1953), L. Fox, 'Early Australian May Days', *Labour History* (No 2, 1962), B. Dickey, 'Parliament and the Trade Unions', *Royal Australian Historical Society* (Vol 47, Part 4, 1961), D. W. Rawson, 'Labour, Socialism and the Working Class', *Australian Journal of Philosophy and History* (Vol 7, No 1, 1961), H. S. Broadhead, 'A Note on J. C. Watson and the Caucus Crisis of 1905', *Australian Journal of Politics and History* (Vol 8, No 1, 1962), L. F. Fitzhardinge, 'W. M. Hughes and the Federal Labor Leadership', *Historical Studies* (No 45, 1965), C. Joyner 'Attempts to Extend Commonwealth Powers, 1908-1919', *Historical Studies* (No 35, 1960), J. B. Welfield, 'That Labor Party and the War, 1914-15', *Armidale and District Historical Society* (No 9, 1966), K. S. Inglis, 'The Australians at Gallipoli', *Historical Studies* (Nos 54-5, April & October, 1970), P.J. Rushton, 'Revolutionary Ideology of the I.W.W. in Australia', *Historical Studies* (No 59, October 1972), W. R. Louis, 'Australia and the German Colonies in the Pacific', *Journal of Modern History* (No 4, 1966), R. C. Thompson, 'The Labour Party and Australian Imperialism in the Pacific, 1901-1919', *Labour History* (No 23, 1972), C. Joyner, 'W. M. Hughes and the Powers Referendum of 1919', *Australian Journal of Politics and History* (Vol 5, No 1, 1959), L. F. Crisp, 'New Light on the Trials and Tribulations of W. M. Hughes, 1920-22', *Historical Studies* (No 37, 1961), B. D. Graham, 'The Place of Finance Committees in Non-Labor Politics, 1910-30', *Australian Journal of Politics and History* (Vol 6, No 1, 1960), P. M. Sales, 'W. M. Hughes and the Chanak Crisis of 1922', *Australian Journal of Politics and History* (Vol 17, No 3, 1971), B. D. Graham, 'The Country Party and the

Formation of the Bruce-Page Ministry', *Historical Studies* (No 37, 1961), P. R. Hart, 'Lyons: Labor Minister—Leader of the U.A.P.', T. Matthews, 'The All For Australia League' and P. Loveday, 'Anti-Political Political Thought', *Labour History* (No 17, 1970), E. M. Andrews, 'The Australian Government and Appeasement', *Australian Journal of Politics and History* (Vol 13, No 1, 1967).

Index

Advisory War Council 13, 182
ALP *see* Australian Labor Party
Anstey, Frank 173
Anzac, a protected word, 150
Anzac Day 150-1
    (1916) 109
    (1918) 147
Anzacs *see* Gallipoli; names of First World War battlefields
Army see Australia, Army
Arnold, Matthew 24, 29
Asquith, Herbert Henry 110-11, 112-13
Australia, Army, 5th Division 113-14
Australia, Constitution see Constitution
Australia and the War Today (Hughes) 176
Australian Freedom League 78
Australian Labor Party 135
    and communism 165
    and conscription 8-9, 127-8, 159
    and expulsion of Hughes 7, 124, 126-7
    Hughes and ALP demonology 18, 159
    Hughes's career in 10-11
    power of party conference 9
    see also Solidarity Labor Party
Australian Metal Company 99-100
Australian Party 12-13, 175
Australian Socialist League 35-7, 65
    Hughes's membership 38-9
Australian War Memorial 148-9
Australian Women's National League 107
Australian Workers' Union 65, 106, 139

Balmain, 16 Beattie Street, Hughes's shop 27-9, 32
Balmain Single Tax League 33
Bank of England 174
Bean, C.E.W., on First World War in Australian history 148
Beattie Street, Balmain 27-9, 32
Bellamy, Edward, Looking Backward 30-1
Brisbane, Hughes's arrival in (1884) 25
Bruce, Stanley Melbourne 12, 162, 168, 169, 171-3
Bullecourt (battlefield) 129

Campbell, Mary Ethel see Hughes, Mary Ethel (2nd wife)
Canberra
    Australian War Memorial 148-9
    foundation stone laid 87
Case for Labor, The, book by Hughes 73
Case for Labor, The, Hughes's column in Daily Telegraph 79-82, 160
Coercion Act (NSW, 1909) 90
Commonwealth Bank 88
Commonwealth Police, formation 12, 142
Commonwealth Shipping Line 10, 113, 168, 172
conscription 78-9
    First World War 8-9, 11-12, 120-8, 140-43
        opposed by Fisher 101
    Second World War 182
Constitution 65-6, 91-3
Cook, Joseph 58, 83, 95-6, 105, 136, 140, 147
Country Party 161, 168, 169
Curtin, John 8, 158, 182
Cutts, Elizabeth see Hughes, Elizabeth (1st wife)

Daily Telegraph
    Hughes column in 171
    The Case for Labor column 79-82, 160
Deakin, Alfred 82-4
Defence of Australia League 176
Democrat, Hughes's letter to the editor 34-5
diggers 151-2

Early Closing Association 70, 77
European fascism, Hughes's warnings against 176-7
Evatt, H.V. 164

Fadden, Arthur 13, 181
federal elections
 (1910) 84-5
 (1913) 88
 (1914) 88-9, 95-6
 (1917) 137
 (1919) 161, 166
 (1922) 166, 168-9
 (1925) 172
 (1928) 172
 (1940) 181
Federal Police *see* Commonwealth Police
federation 11, 65-6, 75-6
First World War 95-147
 1914 election and 95-6
 Anzacs 102-3
 in Australian history 148-51
 Australian support for 95-6, 97-100, 103-4, 132
 propaganda 131-2
 recruitment 98-9, 101, 139, 144-5, 159
  see also conscription
 Second International and 94-5
Fisher, Andrew 72, 73, 92, 93, 107
 and 1910 federal election 84, 85-6
 and First World War 95-6
 as prime minister 117
  in wartime 100-2
 resignation 11, 16, 105
Fitzgerald, J.D. 50, 51
Forrest, Sir John 143-4
Free Trade Party 82, 83
Freedom and Independence for the Golden Lands of Australia
            (Lang) 97
Freedom on the Wallaby (Lawson) 38
Fromelles (battlefield) 113-14

Gallipoli 102-4, 150
 Hughes London speech on 109
Garran, Sir Robert 152, 162
General Labourers' Union 38
George, Henry 10, 33, 39
Golden Gate Hotel 20-1
great strike (1917) 137-8

High Court of Australia 91-2
Higinbotham, George 38
Hitler, Adolf, Hughes's distrust of 178
Holland, Harry 90-1
Holman, William Arthur 65, 108, 120-1, 137, 141
    in Labor Electoral League 46-7
    and New Order 48, 62
    opposed to Hughes in 1918 referendum 141, 142-3
    premier of NSW 101, 106, 120-1
    split from ALP 136, 160
Hughes, Elizabeth (1st wife) 10, 17, 19, 28, 45, 70-1, 72
Hughes, Ethel (daughter) 72, 93
Hughes, Helen (daughter) 109, 147, 152, 175, 177
Hughes, Mary Ethel (2nd wife) 10, 93, 183
Hughes, William (father) 23
Hughes, William Morris
    in ALP demonology 18, 159
    appearance 86, 97, 116
    attorney-general
        (1908-13) 71-3, 87
        (1914-15) 97, 99-100
        (1939-41) 180
    Australia and the World Today 176
    as a barrister 73
    becomes Prime Minister 105
    birth and early life 10, 23
    as a bridge player 133-4
    The Case for Labor (book) 73
    The Case for Labor (newspaper column) 79-82, 160
    death and funeral 153
    early life and career in Australia 25-7
    early life in Sydney 19-22
    elected to NSW Parliament 49-53, 55
    expulsion from Labor Party 124, 126
    expulsion from Nationalist Party 12, 173
    expulsion from United Australia Party 7, 13, 182
    as a farmer 74-5
    as an illusionist 15, 18-19, 27, 118, 134
    as a kitchen man 19-21
    as a Labor Party organiser 41-5
    as 'the little Digger' 152-8
    as a living legend 15, 17-18, 115, 157-8, 170

in London (1916) 108-13
maiden speech in NSW Parliament 58-9
minister for external affairs (1937) 177-8
minister for health (1934) 176
minister for repatriation (1934) 176
in NSW Parliament 56-62, 66-9
as an orator 15-16, 32-3, 35, 48-9, 51-2, 58-9, 68, 97, 104, 111-12, 118, 170
as a parliamentarian 67, 183-4
party political career 7
    see also Australian Labor Party; United Australia Party
political ambitions 72-3
political beliefs 7-8, 38-9, 60-2, 76-8, 79-82, 160-1
    see also conscription; Hughes, William Morris, radicalism; White Australia Policy
political style 24, 67-8, 89, 118-19, 156
as prime minister 115-19
as a pupil teacher in London 23-4
as a raconteur 21-2, 42, 74, 184
    stories 20-1, 22, 26-7, 28, 48, 66-7, 68-9, 75
radicalism 29-31
and referendum campaign (1917) 122-6
resignation and re-appointment as PM 143-4
return from England (1916) 115, 120
socialism 34-40, 64-5
stories *see* Hughes, William Morris, as a raconteur
survival after expulsion from ALP 133-47
vice-president of the executive council (1934) 176
Welshness 25

International Workers of the World 124-5, 137
International Working Men's Association, Second 94-5
Irvine, William 139-40, 146

Japan, Hughes's distrust of 12, 13, 176

Labor Electoral League 40-7
Labor Party see Australian Labor Party
Lang electorate (1894) 49-53
Lang, John Dunmore 97

Latham, Sir John 147, 155, 162, 169
Lawson, Henry, *Freedom on the Wallaby* 38
League of Nations 12, 164
Liberal Party (of Deakin) 83, 84
Liberal Party (of Menzies)
    formation 182
    Hughes joins 7, 13, 182
Lloyd George, David 110-11
    on Hughes's speeches 112-13
Looking Backward (Bellamy) 30-1
Lyons, Joseph 13, 160, 175, 179

McCall, Bill 179-80, 181
McIntosh, Hugh D. 120, 121
Mannix, Daniel, *Archbishop of Melbourne* 128, 132, 141
Marx, Karl 39
Maryborough 26
mateship 43, 150-1
Menzies, Sir Robert 179, 180, 180-1, 182
    on Hughes 13
Merchant Service Guild 74
Messines ridge (battlefield) 129-30
Milner, Alfred, Viscount 109, 110, 111
Mitchell (town) 26
Monash, Sir John 151-2
Morris, William 39
    News from Nowhere 31
Munro-Ferguson, Sir Ronald Crauford 116, 144-5
    on Hughes 116
Murdoch, Keith 110, 176

National Defence League of Australia 77
Nationalist Party 13, 167, 175
    expulsion of Hughes 7, 12
    formation 11, 135-6
Nauru 163
New Guinea 163
New Order (weekly newspaper) 48, 57-8
News from Nowhere (Morris) 31
Niemeyer, Sir Otto 174, 175
Northcliffe, Alfred Harmsworth, Viscount 109-10, 111

Oleander Lodge 21-2, 24

Page, Earle 169, 179
Parliament House, Sydney 54, 55
parliamentary reform (NSW) 56-7, 120
Passchaendale (battlefield) 131
Peace Conference (1919), Hughes's role 10, 12, 154, 155, 162-4
Political Labor League 65
Pozieres (battlefield) 114
price control, proposed referendum (1915) 106-7
Protectionist Party 82, 83

recruitment
    First World War 98-9, 101, 139, 144-5, 159
        see also conscription
referendum campaigns 92-3
    conscription
        1917 campaign 120-8, 159
        1918 campaign 140-3
    see also price control
returned men 149-51
Returned Soldiers and Sailors Imperial League of Australia 140-1
Robinson, W.S. 167-8
Ryan, T.J. 125, 141, 142

Scott, Ernest, on First World War in Australian history 148
Scullin, James 12
Second International 94-5
single tax 10, 33
Socialist Labor Party 65
Solidarity Labor Party 48-53, 62-4
    in NSW Parliament 56-7
Spencer, Herbert 30
squatters 42-3, 54-5
state socialism, defended by Hughes 34-5
strikes
    (1888-92) 37-8
    great strike (1917)
    Hunter Valley (1909) 90
Sydney Wharf Labourers' Union *see* Wharf Labourers' Union
syndicalism 89-90, 106, 124-5

Taylor, John 50, 53
Theodore, E.G. 174
Trades Hall Council, Melbourne, opposition to conscription 123
Trades and Labor Council 37, 40
transcontinental railway 87
Trolley, Draymen and Carters' Union 73, 74, 75

United Australia Party
    expulsion of Hughes 7, 13, 182
    formation 175
    Hughes joins 13
Universal Service League 101

war memorials 148-9
War Precautions Act (Australia, 1914) 97
Waterside Workers' Federation 8, 73, 74, 139
Watt, Sir William 168-9
Wharf Labourers' Union 69-70, 73, 74
    opposition to conscription 122
White Australia Policy 11, 12, 76-7, 164, 165
    and anti-conscription movement 125
working class aspirations 64

Yewen, A.G. 48
Ypres (1917 battlefield) 130-1